GETTING THE KNOW-HOW

Frank Gilbert Roe

GETTING THE KNOW-HOW
Homesteading and Railroading in Early Alberta

Frank Gilbert Roe

Edited by J. P. Regan

Foreword by Lewis G. Thomas

NeWest Press  Edmonton

First Edition

Four chapters in the volume, "Our Sod House," "Log Houses," "Remittance Men," and "A Day in Court," have previously appeared in *Alberta Historical Review.*

Canadian Cataloguing in Publication Data

Roe, Frank Gilbert, 1878-1973
    Getting the know-how

    ISBN 0-920316-45-X (bound). — ISBN 0-920316-43-3 (pbk.)

    1. Roe, Frank Gilbert, 1878-1973. 2. Pioneers - Alberta -
Biography. 3. Grand Trunk Pacific Railway - Biography.
4. British - Alberta - Biography. 5. Frontier and pioneer
life - Alberta. I. Regan, J. P. II. Title.
FC3672.1.R6A33   971.23′02′0924   C82-091244-1
F1078.R63A33

34,127

Cover Photograph: Provincial Archives of Alberta

Credits:
Cover: S. Petterson
Production: N. Miller
Printing: D.W. Friesen and Sons, Altona, Manitoba

Financial Assistance:
Alberta Culture
The Canada Council

NeWest Publishers Limited
#204, 10711 - 107 Avenue
Edmonton, Alberta
Canada   T5H 0W6

Contents

Foreword

When Roe's major work, *The North American Buffalo: A Critical Study of the Species in Its Wild State,* appeared in 1951, W.L. Morton greeted it as "a fine scholarly achievement", "a contribution to Canadian historical studies similar to that of Marcel Giraud's *Le Metis Canadien.*"[1] Roe had already published important articles, "The Extermination of the Buffalo in Western Canada," in the Canadian Historical Review in 1934,[2] "An Unsolved Problem of Canadian History", on the route of the C.P.R., in 1936[3] and "Early Opinions on the Fertile Belt of Western Canada" in 1946.[4] He received an honorary LL.D. from the University of Alberta in 1951 and published his second major work, *The Indian and the Horse,* in 1955, a work that by 1971 had gone into its fourth printing by the University of Oklahoma Press.[5] In 1960 he was elected a Fellow of the Royal Society of Canada, in whose transactions he published five articles of the twenty-five that had been printed by the end of his long life. This was a remarkable scholarly accomplishment for a man who had ended his formal schooling at the age of twelve and spent his working life as a railway engineer.

When Roe died he was negotiating for the publication of his autobiography[6] and this volume is an edited version of two manuscripts he had prepared, one dealing with his early experience as an Alberta homesteader and the other with his railway career, at first with the Grand Trunk Pacific and later with the Canadian National. These manuscripts have much to tell us not only of Roe's own adaptation to the emerging society of the Canadian west but also of the nature of that society.

When Roe arrived with his family at their homestead near Blackfalds in 1894, Alberta was only beginning to feel the full impact of European immigration — European in the broadest sense of the word, for the immigrants were still predominantly from further east in Canada, from the United Kingdom and from the United States. The Alberta of the fur trader and the rancher had fitted easily into the plans of Canada's empire builders, whether English or French in speech. These had designed the imposition upon their splendid hinterland of a polity that was, economically, politically and socially, British in its inspiration but tolerant enough of difference to accomodate cultural variety as long as those of other cultural origins recognized and kept their place. The ideal was essentially an orderly society, structured and hierarchical, open enough not to deny mobility to the exceptionally talented but at the same time able to conserve the values of those who invested in it not only their money but their abilities.

The weakness of this ideal polity lay in its need, if it were to prosper by the intensive agricultural development of its promising and extensive lands, to attract settlers. Settlers from the United Kingdom and the more easterly Canadian provinces might find acceptable the social, economic and political structures that protected the established interests, including those of central Canada. They were, however, open to the influence of a more egalitarian ideal, the ideal of a society based on the small family farm. As the tide of immigration began to flow into Alberta at the turn of the century, the immigrant was likely to be more concerned about land ownership than about land as an investment, about farming as a way of life for himself and his family than about farming as a means of ensuring the profits of business enterprise. Though the boom conditions in the Alberta of the early twentieth century masked the conflict between the two ideals, the recession of 1913 and the outbreak of war in 1914 marked the transformation of Alberta into a society that was less orderly than uneasy.

It was to this changing society that Frank Gilbert Roe responded. His exceptional abilities produced an exceptional response, as his place in the historiography of the west amply attests, but his autobiographical manuscripts also tell us much about the society in which he lived. Indeed it was clearly his intention that they should, and his fundamental purpose was to provide primary source material for the social historian. Even the facts of his life are instructive. The Roes were certainly among those British settlers who saw homesteading as the key to a freer and more abundant life than the industrialized England of the late nineteenth century could offer. Though they were not quickly disillusioned, and indeed coped heroically through the most difficult years, Roe recognized, while still a young man, that the family farm was not likely to be the way in which he would realize the dream of even a modest material prosperity. His decision to seek work with the Grand Trunk Pacific was in a way symbolic. Alberta's development, fuelled by immigration, was in 1908 reaching a peak, and railway development seemed the key to expansion. Though, as his memoir indicates, Roe did not find it easy to establish himself as a railwayman, his decision to leave the farm released him from the bleak poverty that was so often the lot of the immigrant family in the rural Alberta of the twenties and the thirties.

Work with the railway, and the adoption of an urban base, combined to free Roe from the constraints upon intellectual activity imposed by the homestead. His fondness for books, which had always made him seek out the other readers in his vicinity, was fed by the richer resources of a city that, small and remote though it might be, was still a provincial capital and a university town. Indeed the very smallness and remoteness of Edmonton in the years between the wars combined to ease the formation of friendships between town and gown. The university community was also small and its members, perhaps more aware of the provincial and even parochial nature of Edmonton's society than many of their fellow townsmen, were disposed to welcome and encourage someone who, like Roe, shared their interests.

The University of Alberta between the wars was still very conscious of its position as an outpost of Canadian civilization. It was accordingly deeply concerned to maintain its communications with the Canadian heartland of Ontario and Quebec, and beyond that with the United Kingdom. Though some of the eminent members of its faculty were natives of the United States, and more were trained there, their most cherished associations were apt to be with those in the American academic community who still took a trans-Atlantic view. Though Roe was certainly no "Little Englander", and took a skeptical view of imperialism, his mind was formed, by his early experience and by his reading, in a mold that made him fit comfortably into relationships with a community which, in spite of the diversity of its political and philosophical ideas, was inclined to share a common view of the outside world, a view which tried to accommodate both the hierarchical and egalitarian strains in western Canadian society.

Roe moved easily and comfortably in a community of scholars and his interests were broad enough to embrace the sciences as well as the humanities. A man of compelling charm, he made friends among the student body as well as the faculty. He was nominated to the Royal Society of Canada by G.F.G. Stanley and F.E.L. Priestley, undergraduates in history and English respectively at U of A in the late twenties who both had careers of exceptional distinction in their chosen fields. Somewhat earlier than this, in 1941, Roe, through the university's Committee on Honorary Degrees, had been proposed for the degree of Master of Arts, *honoris causa*. To confer what was normally an earned degree rather than the customary Doctorate of Laws, was a most unusual, indeed a unique proposal. It was intended to recognize, as some felt a LL.D. would not, the distinction of Roe's scholarly accomplishments. The motion was carried unanimously at the meeting of the Senate that preceded the Convocation where the degrees were to be awarded.

Unfortunately the other candidate for an honorary degree was the Premier of the province, William Aberhart. The motion put forward by the Committee was rejected by the Senate, an unprecedented break with tradition. The Senate then proceeded to rescind the motion regarding Roe's M.A. and no honorary degrees were awarded at Convocation the following Tuesday.

The Monday after the meeting Roe met, outside the Tuck Shop on 112th Street, George M. Smith, head of the Department of History and Dean of the Faculty of Arts and Science. Smith commiserated with his friend on the events of the past weekend. His beaming equanimity undisturbed, Roe replied, "Ah, well, *Sic transit gloria* Tuesday." The university awarded him an LL.D. in 1951.

Roe's ironic view of the world about him emerges in his memoir even more frequently than in the scholarly publications of his long lifetime. His sharply critical mind made him suspicious of received popular wisdom. He was as impatient with the propagandist who represented the prairie soils as inexhaustible as he was with what he saw as A.S. Morton's unduly charitable judgment of the Hudson's Bay Company. In the chapter in his memoir called "Social Frontiers" he discusses the regional relationships of Alberta in terms of his own experience. What he has to say about relationships, for example, between the Mounted Police, the missionaries and the Indian in southern Alberta, and between the rancher, the cowboy and the sod-buster, is of interest to any student of the formation of Alberta attitudes. His own broad scholarship gives a sophistication to his discussion of the impact of the Ontario settler on the landscape that takes it far beyond the commonly accepted stereotype of the homesteader.

Roe's memoir, and the manuscripts that he left to the University of Victoria upon which this volume is based, are a legacy to the student of the social and cultural history of the Canadian west. Their account of his experience as homesteader and railway man provide an indispensable background for an understanding of his emergence as an internationally recognized authority on aspects of the region's early history.

Lewis G. Thomas
Edmonton, 1981

NOTES:

[1] *Canadian Historical Review,* Vol. XXXII, No. 4, Dec., 1951, pp. 388-9.

[2] *C.H.R.* Vol. XV, No. 1, March 1934, pp. 1-23.

[3] *Canadian Historical Association, Annual Report,* 1936, pp. 66-77.

[4] *C.H.R.* Vol. XXVII, 1946, pp. 131-149.

[5] G.F.G. Stanley, "Biographical Sketch," *Proceedings of the Royal Society of Canada,* 1974, 4th Series, Vol. XII, pp.63-65.

[6] *Ibid,* p. 65.

Preface

Frank Gilbert Roe is best known for his scholarly work on the buffalo: *The North American Buffalo: A Critical Study of the Species in Its Wild State* (University of Toronto Press), and a much more popular work: *The Indian and the Horse* (University of Oklahoma Press). In addition to these important studies Frank Roe was the author of over twenty articles in leading historical and scientific journals such as the *Alberta Historical Review* and *Transactions of the Royal Society of Canada.* There is also a large number of unpublished manuscripts in the Roe Collection at the University of Victoria, two of which formed the basis for this present volume. Other published and unpublished articles include physical and historical geography of western Canada, fiction, history, anthropology, literary critisicm, and a great deal of poetry. One of the interesting sidelights found in much of this writing concerns the attitudes of Europeans *vis-a-vis* the North American Indian. Frank Roe had some interesting concepts in his historical thought — for example he calls the Indian the real "old timer" as opposed to the conventional "old timer" of a mere hundred years ago. This view of the Native Indian as someone with prior rights surfaces in much of Roe's writings. This was a fairly uncommon view to hold fifty years ago, but then he was a fairly uncommon person.

Frank Roe was singularly equipped to record the early social history of what is now central Alberta; his experiences as farmer and railroader encompass what are the two most essential elements of early western Canadian life, i.e., grain growing and fast, mass transport. The first sixty-five years of his life thus span the birth and maturity of the agricultural West. He was born in Sheffield, England on August 2, 1878.

His formal education was brutally short coming to an end in 1889 when his father, a tea blender by trade, lost his job and Frank had to work to help support the family. By 1894, as their economic situation worsened, the family decided to emigrate to Canada. They landed in Quebec City on June 17, 1894, and arrived at Red Deer, Alberta July 5, 1894.

The Roes took up a homestead ten miles east of Blackfalds, Alberta, S.W. 30-39-25 west of the 4th Meridian. Like most homesteaders they built a sod house and settled down to survive in an oftentimes hostile environment. That winter Frank's father became lost in a storm and wandered for hours. This experience so weakened him that he died within the month. The rest of the family decided to carry on and Frank Roe continued to farm until 1908. During this period he furthered his education by borrowing from the libraries of neighbours. One of these neighbours, Paul Makepiece, with his small but good library, was only too glad to lend his books. Another source of good literature was the books that were sent by the London correspondent of the *Manchester Guardian* to his brothers who were also close neighbours of the Roes. Frank Roe thus read widely in Shakespeare, Milton, Bunyan and some of the great nineteenth century historians, Gibbon, Carlyle, and Macaulay. The constant reading of these great writers helped in the formation of the semi-classical style that characterizes his work. This reading also helped in the formation of Roe's lifelong interest in history and particularly in social history.

Meanwhile the homesteading did not go well. The wheat crop was hailed out in 1906, and in 1907 there was a very late seeding followed by an early snowfall that flattened the crops. This double disaster convinced Roe to give up the homestead. He was thirty years old by this time and decided to look for other work while he was still young enough to change his occupation. He continued farming for the season of 1908 in order to pay off any outstanding debts; he writes that he "needed a good season before [he] could quit decently." The "good year" of 1908 afforded the opportunity and he made the break. As the railroad was moving west through his territory and was desperate for men Frank Roe became a "Railroader."

Frank Roe began his railway career with the Grand Trunk Railway as a coal shoveller at the Calder Shop,

Edmonton, in August 1909. He worked at other jobs about the shop such as boiler washer and locomotive hostler till July 1910 when he was promoted to fireman on the 'Pioneer', a track-layer working near Prairie Creek, Alberta. By 1919 he had passed his examinations for engineer and had become chairman of the local Grievance Committee. His union position automatically made him a delegate to the General Grievance Committee meeting annually at Winnipeg. Frank Roe was quickly elected Secretary-Treasurer and helped in the drafting of original proposals for the Schedule Agreement covering pay and working conditions for locomotive engineers and firemen which were negotiated with the companies that later became the Canadian National Railways. During the Depression years Frank Roe was forced to start the dreary routine of a spareboard fireman working out of small and isolated terminals all over western Canada. He worked as far east as Rivers, Manitoba, and as far west as Tete Jaune Cache, British Columbia. During these trying years he maintained his interest in the physical geography and social history of western Canada.

From his vantage point high in the cab of his locomotive Roe could see signs of trails over the Prairies, particularly after a light snowfall or when the wind had blown a light covering of snow into all the hollows. His ever increasing interest in these paths and trails combined with his antiquarian interests started him on his research on the North American buffalo. Roe had joined the English Place-Name Society in 1924 and had started to write on the buffalo and buffalo trails by 1926. His first published article, "The 'Wild Animal Path' Origin of Ancient Roads," appeared in *Antiquity* (England) in 1929. His research on the North American buffalo intensified and by 1934 his published articles on the buffalo had begun to appear.

As Frank Roe's interests expanded so did his circle of friends. He met Ernest Thompson Seton through his friendship with Professor William Rowan and D.E. Cameron, Librarian of the University of Alberta. Roe also met W.T. Hornaday, chief zoologist of the Smithsonian Institution whose theory on the part the Indian played in the virtual extermination of the buffalo in the mid-nineteenth century Roe set out to demolish. What particularly incensed him was

Hornaday's almost total condemnation of the Native Indian *vis-a-vis* the buffalo and the refutation of these ideas became somewhat of a crusade for Frank Roe.

When his monumental work on the buffalo was completed D.E. Cameron started his efforts to gain publication for the work; it was accepted by the University of Toronto Press with the first edition appearing in 1951 and the second edition in 1970. Roe's second book, *The Indian and the Horse,* was published by the University of Oklahoma Press in 1955, with the book going into its fourth printing in 1974. In recognition of Frank Roe's wide ranging interests and scientific writings he was awarded an LL.D. by the University of Alberta in 1951. He was later nominated for membership in the Royal Society of Canada by Dr. F.E.L. Priestley and Dr. George F.G. Stanley. After some little debate which appeared to hinge on the advanced age of the candidate, Dr. Roe was duly elected a Fellow of the Royal Society of Canada in 1960. Frank Roe retired from the Canadian National Railways in 1943 and he moved to Victoria, British Columbia where he was reworking his manuscripts and attempting publication of some of them almost to the time of his death. Frank Gilbert Roe died in Victoria on April 11, 1973.

This present volume is an amalgam of two historical/autobiographical essays written at different times and with two slightly different writing styles. The first: "Alberta in the Early Eighteen-Nineties," written in the mid 1940s, was a scholarly work containing copious footnotes. The second essay: "That's How It Seemed to Be: An Autobiographical Essay," possibly dating from the early 1960s, was written in a much more informal manner. This change was probably in answer to critics who claimed that his writings were scholarly to the point of being pedantic. However, both essays covered similar areas with the major difference being found in the large amount of purely autobiographical material in the second work. My main task was to alter as little as possible Frank Roe's reminiscences of early Alberta. This entailed a comparatively small amount of rewriting necessary to supply continuity and bridging — unavoidable when two substantial essays were being condensed. The other major change to the original texts was to bring the punctuation closer to modern usage;

hopefully this was done in such a way as to change neither the letter nor the spirit of Frank Roe's work or thought.

My objectives in editing these essays were, first to preserve a small segment of the social history of early Alberta, and, second, to supply a framework in which all the writings of Frank Roe coud be placed. It is a simple matter to refer to any history text to find keystone facts of conventional history. It is much more difficult to discover what the early homesteader thought about his life as a farmer, or how it was to work on a rapidly expanding and early rail system. This type of social and industrial history must be preserved and disseminated in order to fully understand our country today. This is what Frank Roe was attempting to do when he wrote his essays — as he said to his fireman on the completion of his last run into Edmonton on the C.N.R.: "I've got about four books to write." This is one of them.

James Patrick Regan

I wish to thank all the people who helped in the compilation of this volume. Special thanks must go to Alan Artibise, Professor of History and Howard Gerwing, Special Collections librarian, both of the University of Victoria. I am also grateful to Georgina Lewis, history editor of NeWest Press for her suggestions and advice which were always welcome. I am particularly grateful to Christopher Petter, archivist at the University of Victoria, whose initial encouragement and continual assistance helped more than anything else to make this volume possible.

I also wish to acknowledge my indebtedness to the Explorations Program of The Canada Council for its generous grant and to the University of Victoria for the use of the manuscripts and photographs in the Frank Gilbert Roe Collection.

J.P.R.

1
Westward Ho!

It was 1894 and the decision had been made — we would emigrate to Canada. My father had just been told by his employer that he was too old for further employment at age sixty-two so we were to seek our fortune elsewhere. My elder brother had preceded us to Canada, Manitoba, and had been back for a visit in 1889. His optimism had been remembered and also served to whet my mother's determination to go to Canada.

Our resources were slender enough. Beyond one or two tables, whose four legs girt around with stout sacking and cording made very manageable bales, we took little more than clothing and bedding. Furniture in a workingman's home in 1894 did not contain many collectors pieces but we had entertained one angel unawares. Chippendale was then a word unknown to our ears but the lure of its possession, as per advertisement, touched off a fight to the finish between a dealer and a parson from the local parish which more than paid the entire expenses of the sale. A distant relative had left my father a small legacy, less than £50 after legacy duty was paid, and a valued friend lent him two or three small sums totalling about $350 in all; it was this latter sum that I was happy to repay nearly twenty years later. I myself was able to make a small contribution to the joint effort. My mother had insisted upon a shilling a week being set aside from my wages in my name. From this provident fund I paid my own fare from Liverpool to Winnipeg: £6. 9s. 4d, about $32. This included board for ten days on the ship; tips would cost as much today.

We had however one prime consideration. We knew exactly where we were going. Everybody knew that Kent was the "Garden of England." We'd heard or read somewhere or other that the Lothians were the Garden of Scotland. We had been told that our prospective destination — the Red Deer district, half-way between **Calgary and Edmonton — was the** Garden of Alberta, as it may fairly claim to be. So we knew precisely what to expect, and were proportionately elated at the prospect.

In one respect, at any rate, the good ship S.S. Parisian of the Allan Line, "their crack boat," was a perfect exemplification of Liberty, Equality, and Fraternity, as befitted a new land. We reached our destination just as quickly as any other of the ship's passengers or crew. Having said this much, however, commendation must pause. I have never discovered just why the third class was dubbed the "steerage" unless the term was meant to convey a deliberately contemptuous connotation. The company's quoted descriptions of its third-class accommodations from the pens of first-class passengers might be defined as masterpieces of either understatement or over-statement. The food was plentiful enough but it was shovelled out, everything on one plate, in a fashion not likely to tempt stomachs already deteriorated by *mal-de mer*. There was one alleviation which was appreciated by a growing and eternally hungry lad who might have had to flee incontinently from the official board. A large canvas sack hung at the entrance to each 'pen'! This was kept filled with small loaves about three inches across which were replenished frequently. These loaves were for the purpose of refilling stomachs whose latest meal was lost. The expert advice was to keep something on our tummies at all times. This device enabled us to co-operate in some measure — there was no butter to this unofficial life-saver but I don't think we missed it.

But the sleeping quarters! These needed the pen of a Kipling to do them justice. There was no door and you entered from the main passageway to a space measuring twenty-four **feet by eighteen feet. This area was almost completely taken up** with bunks with the space between these bunks only some twenty-four or thirty inches wide. Along this tiny passageway the bunks ran, the sleepers lay feet-to-feet on either side with a **widish board and nothing else to divide one sleeping section** from another. You would be kind to call them bunks and I believe there were eight lower and eight upper in all. Nobody

2

undressed for there was no separation of ages or sexes; we consoled ourselves with the reflection that it could not last forever and that meantime we were journeying to our destinations just as fast as the most luxuriously accommodated in the ship. We spread ourselves on our improvised 'beds' as best we could and sooner or later another morning dawned. We were addressed on the Sunday by a passenger-padre who seemed unable to conceal his condescension in bending to our level.

The following Sunday, June 17, 1894, we awoke to find ourselves docked in the port of Quebec which was 'Canada' to the steerage passengers. I felt a mild astonishment at finding **Canadians looked very much like other people. We had no** opportunity for even the briefest exploration, being told that the boat-train for Montreal might leave at any time. Actually we didn't leave until mid-afternoon. *En route* we were greatly entertained by the spectacle at Portneuf, Terrebonne, and other strange sounding places of what seemed like the entire village population who together with their *cure* were at the station to see the train go by.

Spiritually, as one may say, Montreal was not for us. Apart from details of architecture and the like, one fine city with handsome streets containing such things as bookshops, spacious hotels, and marvellously fashionable stores, together with beautiful to gorgeous churches, was very much like another with similar amentities. Being Sunday, in those dear dead days beyond recall when the C.P.R. started no trains out **on a Sunday, we had to kick our heels around until the** Monday evening. We had grown up in a society where the fellow who missed the 9:38 caught the 11:30, and the wait, where the only refuge from the scorching streets was the bare, comfortless Waiting Room at Windsor Station, seemed interminable.

We found our place in one of those Colonist Cars so **rapturously extolled, once again by first-class sleeper lyricists,** and settled ourselves on the bare slats for three nights as philosophically as we could. Thence to Winnipeg our chief interest was in greeting many places which by dint of intensive study of immigration literature had become extremely familiar but which we recognized instinctively as belonging to other worlds than ours. Our early morning vision of the prairie lands east of Winnipeg was our earliest glimpse of that 'West' to which we had given our allegiance. We were nearly at Winnipeg and with the exception of the midsummer sunrise passage around the North Shore of Lake Superior—a panorama of matchless beauty — the endless miles that we had travelled seemed a waste howling wilderness.

Winnipeg, as we saw it that cloudless midsummer morning in 1894, June 21, the longest day in the year, seemed a curious conglomeration of the ancient and the modern. It had railways, of course, which go a long way to modernize any city particularly to those who have waited long and anxiously for their coming. These tracks ran through the streets and we, who had never looked at a railway track in our lives other than over a wall or through a fence, found this difficult to assimilate. There were also street-cars, or rather a 'Street-Railway' on which I rode that evening through a waste of luxuriantly high grasses even then called River Avenue.

Main Street was as yet unpaved, and we had the opportunity of noting, after a heavy rain, the legendary power of Winnipeg 'gumbo' to pull the shoes off one's feet. I saw it actually happen to a lady and she was wearing laced shoes at that. There were, of course, no automobiles but I saw what surely must have been one of the very latest generations of Red River carts, drawn by a single ox, pursuing its shrieking way. Its Indian or Metis accompaniments were by no means rare while farmers with hay racks or loads of poles were familiar enough at any time.

My eldest brother met us at the station in all the assured position of 'twenty years and five in the country'. On rising that morning I had bedecked myself as beseemed a gentleman in collar and tie. My brother scorned such gauds and in answer to my mother's shocked disapproval and my own (unspoken) surprise, he explained that 'nobody wore such things out here'. I wondered at the time — and still do — if this was just another way of saying that he didn't wear them or hadn't them to wear. Being desirous of becoming a Canadian, and to be taken for one at the earliest possible moment, these secret doubts did not prevent me from joining the emancipated then and there. I have often wondered just what our parents' earliest Canadian friends must have thought of us.

We were held at Winnipeg, where our original tickets

expired, for several days while my father was fully engaged in persuading the C.P.R. to endorse the English agent's ebullient optimisms *re* 'cent a mile' rates into plain sober fact. In the light of later knowledge I marvel that he accomplished it at all. As it happened we learned of his success less than an hour before the C.P.R. Number One westbound was due to leave. Losing this connection entailed, in those days, a three day stop-over in Calgary which our parents could ill afford. Knowing this we made a lightning change act of our packing.

As on our initial run to Winnipeg, our chief interest was in identifying this or that place from our immigration literature. As we worked our way west to the 'baldheaded prairies' we saw at least one exciting link with the past. There still remained at Maple Creek a long stack of bleaching buffalo bones alongside the track. The alkali plains and the long dessicated ridges of the Missouri Coteau might rather have daunted us had we not known how utterly different was the destination to which we were bound. We were going to the Garden of Alberta.

Calgary, then as now, was the jumping off place for Red Deer in what was then 'Northern' and is now called Central Alberta. We reached the city in the small hours and had little enough time for sight-seeing as we were due to leave again at 8 a.m. Beyond seeing a clean, pleasant-looking, small town of some four or five thousand — as we were proudly told — with the beetling masses of the Rockies in the western distance, the only typical western spectacle we saw was a mounted squadron of the Northwest Mounted Police. They were returning from a morning exercise and wearing their khaki undress; they looked just as we had expected.

Our trip northward on the mixed train was our first really extended view of Alberta by daylight. Our first reaction was one of disillusion and disappointment. Rolling grassy hills, not a tree the thickness of a ramrod or a bush that could have covered a tablecloth. Scarcely one's idea of a garden. In the first fifty miles there were only four houses, no inhabited stations, two boxcars on one of the ten-miles-apart sidings, and not a cultivated field to be seen. The first inhabited station-house was at Olds, fifty miles up; the village apparently had some twenty or thirty buildings. 'Thank God this isn't where we have to get off'. The next town, Innisfail,

Red Deer, 1894

was about twenty miles farther on. In the interval and without knowing it, we had crossed the great demarcation, the borderline between the 'baldheaded prairies', the Great American Desert' of Zebulon Montgomery Pike and the northern scrub and timber, long grass, black-soil territory. At Innisfail there were a few poplar trees scattered about the village; this was getting better but still not quite up to Garden standards. 'Thank God we are not getting off here either'. The next stop was Red Deer and we got off whether we wanted to or not. Our hearts sank — so this hole was the Garden of Alberta. What could its jungles be like?

Red Deer, in the river bottom, is the one place in the entire 200 miles between Calgary and Edmonton from which the surrounding country cannot be seen. The river-flat upon which the town stands was then covered with willow and poplar scrub high enough to lose a man on horseback. The first thing we saw was what proved to be the roof of the Methodist Church (the town had been founded by a Methodist minister) showing above the scrub. Nothing beyond could be seen except the almost precipitous cut-banks of the Red Deer River and the sombre coniferous foliage of the spruce forests. I think all of us, even our Manitoban, felt that we had indeed crossed the Rubicon and stern fate had burnt the bridge. What we should have done had the place not possessed an Immigration Hall I can't imagine, hotels being utterly beyond us. We moved our belongings over to this dismal barrack and one corner of what seemed like a huge bare barn became our home for a space. I'm not sure whether any of us had a bed except the floor.

I had fondly hoped to make one of the land-hunting party that was arranged for us the next day. Alas, at the eleventh hour a gentleman showed up, afterwards a valued neighbour, who as an additional full fare manifestly outbid me. I kicked my heels in a somnolent shack-town with nowhere to go and nothing to do. Had I had the money, I still believe that when the southbound mixed came through on her return trip to Calgary, I would have boarded her and left the Garden of Alberta and the Granary of the Empire to stew in their own juice. I fell asleep at last in that dreary den from sheer exhaustion of body and mind; the next thing I knew was the return of the explorers. They had chosen a quarter-section twenty miles out and I was to go with them on the coming Monday morning. Away went boredom where all bad dreams go.

2

Our Sod House

I really do not know what actually led to the choice of a sod house for our first prairie home in July 1894. No doubt here, as is commonly true, economic necessity was the main factor. Sod houses were not common affairs in northern Alberta. Although a practiced hand could make a very good job of building one, in the nature of things they were less permanent than log or frame houses. I never heard of anyone building them for a permanent choice where other material was readily to be had. They were essentially a creation of the treeless prairies where other raw materials were inaccesible and they were regarded by their builders as temporary substitutes until something more acceptable could take their place.

When the adult members of the family were introduced to their future domain by the land guide, they found that they were not the first to view the promised land. A wandering pilgrim from the western states, a covered wagoner, had been there before them. During his brief stay he had broken what was clearly meant for a firebreak of four or five furrows around the base of a tiny shallow knoll on the level quarter-section. Within this space his tent, wagon, and household goods in general had been stowed for safety from prairie fires. A patch of charred ashes indicated the site of his camp. He had pulled out after a month or so, and the place knew him no more.

Perhaps the departed pilgrim's fire-break turned the thoughts of the newcomers toward sod. During the years in Manitoba the eldest son of our family had heard of the Mennonite sod houses, but I don't think he had ever seen one. It is unlikely that the newly-arrived parents, fresh from

9

England, had any ideas concerning the prairie type of their first prairie home. It was to him they would naturally look for direction on such matters as a much more mature Canadian than any of us.

There was no mention of building with sod on their first enthusiastic return from the land hunt, the trip from which I had been removed by the last minute appearance of an additional paying passenger for the landguide's democrat. Since the guide had approached the place from the most remote angle from the old camp, possibly none of them even saw the spot until actually taking possession. The economic urge was an imperative one. After paying the homestead fee and the landguide's charges, the family had almost exactly ten dollars. Nor was this offset by teams, ploughs, wagons, or dairy stock, objects which rendered many a beginner a relatively well-to-do man.

Then, too, log timber suitable for building proved to be some distance away, and not easy of access in summer time. The nearest lumber-yards, even had funds permitted, were respectively eleven and twenty miles distant. And at this season of the year people were too busy breaking new land or preparing for early hay-making to embark upon such winter occupations as logging, or even freighting, for any less inducement than spot cash. Perhaps in the existing circumstances there wasn't much choice in the matter.

Viewed in the light of later knowledge, our building material left something to be desired. To us sod was sod. In later years, we learned a considerable amount of sod house lore from neighbours who had lived in them in Nebraska and the Dakotas. These states furnished a sod of a peculiarly hard and enduring character not precisely equalled by anything our informants could discover in our own locality. The sod should properly be broken at a particular season of the year, late autumn being the best, when no rain has fallen for a considerable time. It should be built into the walls as quickly afterward as possible. Such a sod as this, when carefully shaved off to a level face, could actually be plastered.

Such competent critical advisers were not to be had, however, when we were building. With one exception, all our immediate neighbours were from eastern Canada. While they were mostly skilled woodsmen, they knew no more about

10

building with sod than we did. Besides, being English and hence scarcely responsible for our actions, their common reaction was suggestive of damning with faint praise: "We-ell, I guess it'll be warm, anyway." Apart from that important saving clause, the log-building forest psychology of native woodsmen could see no form nor comeliness in a habitation of sod.

Being thus completely unversed in the art of sod house construction, there was nothing to disturb our comfortable conviction that sod was sod. Quite untroubled by any qualms, we turned to the soft rich black sod of the firebreak, which lay ready to our hands. Fortunately the breaking ploughs of 1894, in the hands of a skilled ploughman, could go from one end of a field to the other without breaking the 'furrow-slice'. As it was, it frequently proved convenient to carry our sods, commonly two feet in length and grass-side down, on a short piece of board. From there they could be slid into position with less danger of them cracking in our hands.

We first decided to dig out a couple of feet of soil inside the walls. This was done after building up an equal height of sod wall all around to prevent our excavated soil from falling in again. Although this later proved to be really necessary, there is a lingering suspicion that laziness (perhaps 'labour-saving' is a more dignified term) had something to do with our decision at the moment. There would be so much less wall to build up!

The little knoll, no more than a tiny swelling, facilitated this and in a sense visibly justified this action. But it also became apparent after a time that in addition to greater warmth and comfort it would have been virtually impossible to have a durable and clean earthen floor without going down through the soft fertile loam to the harder clay sub-soil below. We therefore dug out an area eighteen feet by twelve, the inside dimensions of our new home-to-be, laying the inner edges of our sod walls flush with the edges of the excavation.

The northern and eastern walls were to be windowless. In these it was therefore feasible to build up a considerable section of the wall self-supporting, laying the sod like brickwork with the joints broken and staggered. But the doorway in the southern end and the small window on the western side brought us face to face with the question of wall plates to support the roof, and further support for these themselves in turn. The roof would have to be of thin, dry, straight poles two to three inches thick, laid closely from ridge to eaves and nailed there for greater rigidity. The roof was also of sod over a good thickness of coarse slough hay, with a generous top dressing of clay over all to cover the joints in the sod. The hay was laid next to the poles to reduce the dust; the roof as a whole, therefore, was clearly the heaviest feature in the work. Even a wallplate of broad plank the full width of the fourteen-inch sod wall could hardly have carried such a weight without thrusting out the wall upon which it rested and, in any case, we had no plank. The only sawmill material in the entire construction was in the door and window frames and in the door itself.

We evolved a skeleton framework of light poles from the woods. The plates — themselves light poles — were supported along the two long sides by posts at intervals, roughly resembling in principle the studding of a frame house. These were set in a little, to be flush with the inner face of the sod wall, the sods at those points being channelled in a little to make them fit closely. The ridge pole, the largest piece of all, was held in position by a stout post at either end and by a third post halfway along. This last post was of dry fire-killed poplar from which the bark had naturally cracked and fallen off. In time most of it became beautifully polished as the family rubbed past it to and fro. The only exception was the area near to ground level which belonged to the family cat. This valued feline, who in a world where demand exceeded supply had been "spoken for" even before birth, kept her claws in working order by a daily drill that did not necessitate her leaving the congenial neighbourhood of the stove.

Had we known where to find them, we could have reduced the weight of the roof by the use of dry roof poles. As things were, every piece of the original framework was green. In order to stiffen our frame as much as possible, each roof pole was firmly nailed to plate and ridge pole at either end instead of being held in position by the weight of sods and clay. Roof and wall were thus independent of one another so it was possible for the sod wall to settle slightly away from the roof. This was met by stuffing into the crevices a sufficiently thick filling of sod and packing the tiny semi-circular crannies

Pioneers outside sod shack, 1907-08

between the poles with rags and paper. The final finishing was the fitting of the door frame and the small window. The green pole studding was placed at the distances necessary to make a snug fit for the frames which were then securely nailed in place. All crevices were then stuffed up tightly.

When the essential work on walls and roof was completed the soil that had been thrown out of the excavation was banked up against the walls. At the northern end where the small knoll was the highest and the digging consequently the deepest, this made what orators call a "really significant contribution." However, the outer walls at no point stood much more than four feet above the surrounding prairie level as the inside clearance at the eaves was only six feet. These features gave additional stability to the walls and increased the portion of the surface that was absolutely windproof. The banking furthermore furnished immensely improved drainage away from the walls.

Before winter set in a small porch about six feet in depth was built on the southern end. This was also of sod construction. It had a door of its own, placed at right-angles to the main house door, to hinder any direct draught from the bitter southeast winds. More than one visitor told us that when approaching the little home in stormy weather, and particularly from the north, he had no suspicion that he was close to a dwelling until he drew near enough to detect the stovepipe showing above the roof. Their surprise was no wise lessened on going indoors. The first astonishment had been on finding a dwelling house. The second — and greater — was at finding a home!

From the first we intended our sod house to be merely a temporary makeshift, partly from a desire to be as good as our neighbours. In the following winter we got out timber for a log home. We put this up and entered into residence in the fall of 1895. The sod building survived for a time as a henroost, but prairie loam sod was fatal to any very long continuance. It only lasted about another year.

I took my wife to see the old homestead, fifty years exactly to the day after my own first sight of the scene. A railroad fill now ran across the site of my mother's garden, and the scene was much changed. Fields stood where long ago had been wood; little bluffs and spinneys of woody growth had

14

replaced open pot holes of swamp or gumbo. Yet in so far as one could detect, the site of our sod house had not been disturbed by railroad grading. But the rains and frosts of half a century had done their work in the meantime. I went down on my hands and knees and felt to see if I could discover any trace of depression or shoulder, but I could not identify the least vestige of our former home.

3

The Pioneer Homemaker

Men may build a house. It takes a woman to make a home. Ours was blessed with a real homemaker.

My mother was a born pioneer. Nor was this to be ascribed to the venturesome urge of youth, for she was no longer young. She scarcely could be with her range of recollection, which on her reminiscent days, was a pageant of Coventry history of over half a century recounted from an amazingly tenacious memory. As a child, escaped from home for the purpose, she had witnessed the public execution of a woman in the last year (1849) in which such spectacles were seen in England, and in common with many Coventry children she was quite familiar by sight with a certain Miss Mary Ann Evans who later became known to a larger world as George Eliot. She clearly recalled the death of the Duke of Wellington (1852), and her old minister's funeral text. She also recalled a red-letter day in 1858 when she saw the Queen and the Prince Consort drive up quite unattended to visit the ancient castle at Kenilworth, a stone's throw across the way from the old inn which was her home. Actually she was fifty-five years old on the day on which she entered into her earthly kingdom. It cannot be made too clearly understood that in her estimation the sod house, standing on its own acres and ours, was no step down in the world but a most decided step up.

It will, one may hope, have been made plain that it was not from any poverty of ideas that such a woman found rest in her soul in the new sphere. Without some historical knowledge of the eviction of the disinherited English peasantry from those ancient "common fields" which once, as their name indicates, were common to themselves conjointly with other classes, it is difficult to realize their passionate longing. The land was to them as the very marrow of their bones. Beyond measure, to such people the possession of acres of their own over which they could stride at will outweighed everything that could be thrown into the scales against it. This was their kingdom and even a sod house could become as a royal palace and she set about to make it one.

Of luxuries, as the term is commonly understood, the little home had none and she was quite prepared to do without them. She had long been accustomed to other luxuries that would more than compensate; the kind word, the gentle touch, the generous appreciation, the loving reverence, the perfect trust. These did not fail her now nor, I think, at any time during her well-nigh four score years and ten. But the little knick-knacks that most women love to have about them — these had to wait.

In a single room, eighteen feet by twelve, space is assuredly at a premium. There was neither overmantel, plate-rail nor dressing table. The bed occupied one corner, built bunk fashion upper and lower, and curtained off at night. The parents took the lower, the two boys the upper. The kitchen table from England was not "the table." Its two leaves had been turned up and fastened about with cleats and in this form, metamorphosed into a packing case and corded with a cover of stout sacking, its cargo of precious household goods and chattels had survived the perils of the trip. It now reigned supreme beneath the little window, a veritable autocrat of the breakfast tables of mankind. It was dining table, kitchen sink, workbench, and writing desk, and, not infrequently before the first church services made their appearance amongst us, a reading lectern.

The cookstove stood with its back to the wall, opposite the window, with space behind, in default of a regular wood-box at first, to hold the wood for the night. I cannot recall precisely whether we had one chair apiece or not. If we did I am rather puzzled to know where we could have stowed them. I know that my own favorite seat was a long low box we had brought from England. This was placed by the stove on the inner side away from the door, and on which the oven door was permanently wired tight. This ex-packing case was covered with a folded rug which served as a cushion; it was just the right height for holding a largish book on one's knee more conveniently than a chair.

Apart from tables and chairs the furniture was home-made or home-adapted. The framework of the bunk-bedstead was of dry poplar poles, peeled by fire. Lengths of board nailed across served, or perhaps in some instances failed to serve, the purposes of a spring mattress. On these was laid a deep pile of coarse slough hay, and on this the feather bed.

The cupboards were ex-packing cases or made from such. The largest was deep enough that half, or two-thirds, made the body, while the remainder furnished lumber for shelves and doors. Other cases were stood one on another in the furthest corner, serving as linen closets or china cupboards housing the precious possessions.

From this description there may seem but little in which the exultant pride of ownership could identify as much of a "palace." But these matters were merely the naked framework, the raw material for a home. They were softened and beautified by the loving touch of the expert; that mysterious something which in this woman's province itself can turn a hat or gown into a creation. The bare walls of sod were hidden away from sight, with building paper being used on the more exposed portions, and newspaper where less rubbing was likely to occur. These not only made for brightness in the aesthetic sense, but vastly increased the power of one little window to light the place. The window itself had a neat blind and tiny curtains, that clothed its nakedness with grace.

Similarly, the corners of the bunk-bedstead were draped with long crimson hangings of dignified order, reaching from roof to floor for both beds. These conferred almost the austere solemnity of a Georgian four-poster. My mother's table, in the leisured portion of its days, was seldom without a parlourish type of tablecloth. The cupboards were relieved of their bareness by mats, tops, worked cloths, runners, or doilies on which a book or some articles of utility or ornament were arranged.

It was not very long before the earthen floor became trampled and baked into a consistent firmness that could be swept. Certain parts of the floor could not be conveniently covered but the major portions were and my mother's feet never touched the bare earth. Where she stood at her daily tasks she had a thick knitted hearth rug of her own make. Similar rugs of smaller size were spread before the bed or where we habitually sat. This reduced the grinding action of shoes to a minimum and helped to keep down the dust. On the walls a few attractive 'Christmas numbers' broke the monotony and enhanced the general effect. Warmth, geniality, cleanliness, and tidiness spelled comfort and comfort spells home.

Beyond doubt contrast played some part in creating an impression. Travellers must have experienced a subconscious influence of contrast, on passing from the rather mean exterior to the sweetness and light within. The vital thing is that this feeling also remained with us. Either the force of contrast never weakened or some other feeling persisted within us after this had gone.

Perhaps contrast exhibited its crowning manifestation on our first Christmas Day in Alberta. There were seven of us at the feast. The little table would only hold six so I sat on the low box. Our guests were three English bachelor neighbours living together a couple of miles away. My mother's table might have confronted the much more exacting standards of later years without fear of humiliation. She had explored her small reserves of hidden treasure; some damask, a modicum of old Sheffield plate, and a trifle even of cut glass had survived the perils of the Great Trek and were present on her board. These accessories were not esteemed less highly because of a most excellent dinner or even by the circumstance that the guests had never seen them on the same table before. One of the guests wondered if "in the length and breadth of the land had another such dinner ever been served so royally in a sodhouse before."

I have said something of the manner in which my mother gave herself to her new life and in some respects this was a fulfilment of her life in England. In the last of her English homes in which she had opportunity to till the soil, she had fenced her own little garden and built a tiny greenhouse. Some potentialities of the new life, then, were not completely new to her. Also, it is nothing remarkable that her first Alberta hen, bought as a complete stranger with her setting of eggs, should be eating from my mother's hand before twenty-four hours had passed and as she ever afterwards continued to do. The same may be said of other domestic animals indoors and out: all these were pets. On her return from a trip to England, long after the sod house era, her three cats heard her voice afar off and tore down the trail to greet her. And one bright Sunday morning, three of our pigs followed her a goodly distance along the woodland trail to church until an unsympathetic fence intervened. The three coyotes that followed her home along the same way one evening may have been moved by other promptings.

My mother influenced us in many ways. Her reaching out to a new life, her determination to like everything in her new life, had a profound influence on us. Neither hardship nor discouragement ever seemed to daunt her. For instance, sod roofs, particularly after the first year's newness had passed, were prone to leak in the summer downpours. The ideal sod and clay roof belonged to an old-timer in our neighbourhood; this roof was about three feet thick. This gentleman endured a three-day rain with unruffled composure. Under these conditions he stayed dry; after three days he moved his belongings out of doors while the roof 'rained' inside to its heart's content. While this was one answer to the problem of rain we preferred another solution; we exchanged 'government shingles' for the ordinary wooden ones. I shall never forget how eagerly we waited for the first real rain and with what exultant glee we awoke that June morning. The sound of downpour might well wake us, for on a sod and clay roof a heavy rain produced a low rumble, not unlike a long freight crossing a trestle. The new roof, only two inches thick, gave forth a din like ten thousand tin pans banging in a boiler shop. We lived under our old sod roof for nine summers, both in our sod house and later in our sod-roofed abode, until my mother was drawing nigh to sixty-four years.

My mother took all this in her stride and I have not the least doubt that early Alberta had many such women but their worth and efforts are too often overlooked in the chronicles of the early years. Of their kind it was well said that the righteous should be held in everlasting remembrance.

4

Log Houses

If Alberta eighty years ago was no land of frame barns, it certainly was a community of log houses. In those days, when central heating was completely outside the orbit of a homesteader's range of thought, I knew men who, in the more exposed situations, actually preferred a log house rather than a less-than-perfectly finished frame one. I must say that I never entered any of the very few early frame houses in the rural areas without thinking what dismal comfortless dens they appeared to be. Perhaps the very circumstance of a frame house pitched our expectations unreasonably high. They were very seldom painted, and commonly not lath-and-plastered until a much later day. Generally they were unfinished also to anything like the degree necessary to make a winter home snug under conditions of stove heating. In fact they had a name for being cold. As a general point of view one might say that we pitied the frame house dweller who was driven to it in a timberless country, and scorned the one who had built of frame because a log house wasn't good enough for him.

It has frequently been observed that a man's log house was quite manifestly the poorest building on his place, his barns and stabling being noticeably superior. This circumstance has given rise to somewhat caustic comment on a type of farmer who was much more concerned about his livestock than about his wife. Nobody who knows the farm will deny that such men existed. Yet to accept this as a sort of blanket explanation for any and every example of such conditions would be grossly unjust. Experience leads me to suggest another frequently more authentic, and much less invidious reason. This was actually the case on my own homestead.

My log home for many years was really and truly the poorest log building on the place, but this was for good reason. I was actually at work on the quarter-section, getting out a set of logs for a house and peeling them, as well as digging a cellar and breaking a small patch of about four acres for some two months before we could "scare up" the ten dollars for the homestead entry fee which should make the place mine. Although I had had my eye on the place for some time prior to attaining the homestead age of eighteen, I had been over it only once or twice previously. In the early spring of 1897 I made a more careful visit of examination. This and its purpose were a secret, known only to my mother and myself. It was not at all uncommon for a settler in straits for cash to go ahead and "squat" on a homestead. Even the dominion land regulations, not to say customary local opinion, regarded him as being entitled to first choice. Where one could not immediately enter into bona fide residence by making his definite home there (which was then my precise situation), the putting up of even the bare walls of a shack was considered in local opinion to make the place one's own *de facto* in a way that nothing else could do quite so authoritatively.

The bounds of the place ran into the timber and had later to be carefully squared and paralleled by myself. On this first visit of exploration I knew nothing of them beyond the merest guesswork. Of the timbered land behind I knew even less. Our own timber cruising had been in other directions. On the very threshold of my approach to the quarter I came across a clump of poplars. They were not overly straight, but they were large enough and long enough for logs, and sufficient to make a set. They were only some quarter of a mile from the approximate place where I decided to raise the shack. I wasted no time looking for better logs anywhere else. I got these down, hauled them to the site and had them peeled, my cellar dug, and my little field broken before I paid my homestead fee and was granted formal entry rights.

I have reason to know that in many cases this was the actual experience of men who threw up their first shack from such timber as offered itself close at hand. I have no doubt whatever, judging from my own experience — it was in fact a homestead truism — that it was commonly not possible to erect the later mansion of one's dream until long after the

Frank Roe's log cabin on his homestead, c. 1900

presaged time. In the meanwhile, a wider knowledge of the neighbouring timber resources, and somewhat less imperative conditions of time enabled them to build a better structure for stabling than the one they dwelt in.

It is a curious historical fact that the Americo-Canadian log house of almost universal English-speaking choice, does not derive from the English-speaking lands. The old English 'timbered house', of which there are examples remaining which go back at least to the fourteenth century (and doubtless was no new fashion then), as well as very early ones in New England, is perhaps best perpetuated on this continent by the great log-framed barns of eastern Canada and the New England states. The eminent American historian, John Fiske, has emphasized this resemblance in portions of Suffolk (whence many Pilgrims came) and New England. In either land you might well think yourself in the other.

The Western log house built of logs laid horizontally one above another is said to be of Scandinavian-Russian origin; or more shortly, I suppose, of Baltic origin. I am not competent to question this. I believe that its appearance in the Canadian West is traceable to the French-Canadians, wherever they may have obtained it. The earliest English-speaking fur traders into what is now Alberta particularly noted that the "French Houses" which they found up the Saskatchewan were built "log on log." The specific mention in this manner is proof in itself of an unfamiliar style. Anthony Henday (1754-55), an Englishman by birth, says this of Fort Poskoyac or Pasquia, The Pas of today. Matthew Cocking (1772-73) says the same of Nipawi, further up the river. The builder of this latter house is known to have been a Frenchman, Francois le Blanc, 1768. It is also on record that in order to assist his Red River settlers, a band of expert French-Canadian axemen were intended to have been sent from Montreal by Lord Selkirk; but the rival Nor-Westers prevented it.

As late as 1894, almost all the hewn and dovetailed log houses in our immediate neighbourhood were put up by the same man, a French Metis named Pouchon or Poucher (locally "Po-shaw"). This past master did not even live in the locality, but was some twenty miles away up the Blindman River. It was considered, even by many Canadians among our neighbours, partly resourceful ingenuity and partly arrogant

24

conceit to think of doing one's own dovetailing. "You'd better get old Poshaw if you want a good job. . . . " I think it was the advent of the Americans in force that overthrew this idol-worship. After this, doing one's own log-work was taken for granted.

I saw one or two specimens of a style of log building which was said to have been derived from the Russians, and very commonly followed in Alaska. The man who practised it in our immediate neighbourhood was an old Klondiker, a Michigander — the American counterpart of the Canadian who is "born with an axe in his hands." Instead of hewing the vertical faces of the logs (inside and outside), this man hewed the top and bottom faces. In Alaska and the Yukon the practice was then to spread the upper surface of the previous log evenly with moss to a thickness of some two inches or more. The dovetails were cut just deeply enough to preclude the log riding anywhere but at the corners. The weight of the log bedded the moss tight and hard, and the moss "ends" furnished a grip for the plastering. This made a close, windproof joint. The same man hewed his walls on the inside as well; and this method struck me as one requiring really large *conifera* with a minimum of taper. I have somewhere read that the North-West Mounted Police, when they built their fort in the Yukon, selected for convenience the smallest Banksian pine they could find; which trimmed thirty-six feet long and ten inches square. The trees must have been grand specimens to begin with.

I have often suspected that the famous Hudson's Bay style of log construction originated as the result of ignorance and inexperience which crystallized into a custom and then into a rigid convention. This method consisted of sinking pairs of huge posts or piles at intervals and dropping the short lengths of log between them. We learn that the Songhee Indians at Victoria undertook to cut an immense number of 22-foot logs for James Douglas for the building of a new fort in 1843; perhaps this gives us the standard length. Men from Stornoway and the Orkneys would probably have little knowledge of different styles of logwork; neither was there any native type among the Metis voyageurs on either side, in so far as historical evidence and later preferences serve to indicate. I have often seen much more ingenious and workmanlike tricks practised by single-handed homesteaders who had to build with short logs when they couldn't get enough long ones, and profiting by such examples I have done likewise.

Some log houses I have seen were manifestly labours of love, marvels of beautiful workmanship, often built with nothing but an axe for a tool-kit. I recall one built by an old bachelor French-Canadian from Quebec. The only nails in the thing were in the door and possibly to hold the floor down. Everything inside and out was peeled and hewn. His very roof-poles were individually peeled, between 150 and 200 of them! The floor was of puncheons — small sticks of not more than six inches diameter, split and hewn smooth on the flat side. Even the hinges of old Joe's door were home-made of wood; two bulging knots or elbows with inch holes bored through the protruding parts, and a thin, stiff rod of spruce running through both and equalizing the strain. They were well greased and worked silently and efficiently. That house, fresh from his hand as I saw it in 1895, should have been placed in a museum.

The Russian settlers also did some very fine work, but their log houses followed a radically different principle. So far as logs were concerned, they made no pretence either of hunting up what we should have termed good logs, nor of erecting them in similar fashion. Their logs were big straight green poles — four or five inches thick was ample. they were peeled in June (when such things must be done to make a good job) and built up with sufficient space between them to admit one's hand. A long unbroken span of wall would be stiffened once, perhaps twice, with pegs driven into auger-holes above and below. In this condition, the whole erection from ground to peak was left for a year to dry thoroughly. When dry the logs were completely covered beyond sight or suspicion with well-mixed mud containing a liberal mixture of coarse grass. This was "keyed" between the logs into a combined and homogeneous mass, precisely as a plasterer keys his plaster behind the lath. A thatched roof was the next feature. The thatch was likewise of the coarse rushy slough grass, bound into even bundles and pegged down. The structure was entirely without nails, except possibly in the making of the door.

Cold was unknown in such a building for the stove was

26

actually a brick oven, on the top of which (in the earlier days) the inmates slept. Had ventilation received equal attention, such dwellings would have been almost beyond criticism as winter homes. But the one tiny half-sash window was hermetically sealed for the winter by strips of paper pasted over every joint. The Russian boys were outdoors more, which was a healthy counterbalance, but the mother and the small girls commonly bore complexions the colour of putty.

Something of the feeling behind old Joe's masterpiece came over me when I had a log building on my hands. The thought of a bee, with all the painstaking detail which I loved being turned over to uninterested outsiders, was not merely distasteful but abhorrent. As strength increased and experience widened I realized my own capability to handle these matters without assistance. I decided to reserve them for myself as a pastime job for the long summer evenings after a broiling day. A man in his twenties could tackle weights that would have baffled a lad of eighteen. I had moreover learned many cunning methods of avoiding the crude strains of a straight lift.

I suppose my inner feeling was the constructive urge, the old creative joy of the craftsman who made something with his own hands, that consummation which the piece-and-pattern worker, standing before a belt conveyor, one of an army, a mere cog or pin in a huge imponderable machine, cannot achieve. To me it brought with it a sense of spiritual content second only to the supreme joy of handling a plough in the conquest of the virgin wilderness.

5

Finding Our Feet

In recalling some of our problems in learning the agricultural lore of a new land, I am reminded of a brief conversation with a friend before leaving England. When it became known that we were going to Canada he asked me what we were going to do there. I answered at once, to farm. "But you've no experience of farming, have you?" I replied that we had not "but you don't need experience in Canada. Everybody says that. . . ." He made no reply but changed the subject. I couldn't help thinking it strange that an educated man like himself, who had read and travelled, should be ignorant of something on which all the emigration pamphlets agreed.

It was quite true of course that much of the particular experience of the older lands that had been cropped for centuries was unnecessary in Western Canada. The usages of artificial and chemical fertilizers to enrich the soil and what fertilizers to use for what crops and for which soils, were then quite needless. But new land also has its problems and we had to learn them.

The allegedly inexhaustible fertility of the prairie soils is a myth of the unscrupulous propagandist. They can be exhausted by careless and rapacious farming which has been responsible for the shameless and wicked deterioration of large areas. None the less it is equally true that the virgin soils — most particularly the heavy black loams of the central scrublands — are of an extraordinary richness with a riotous growth that needs to be controlled rather than encouraged and that with care can be maintained at a high level for years.

The principal soils of the prairie lands are of two main types. The southeastern portion of the Alberta territory, the

28

short-grass 'baldheaded plains', has a chocolate soil, much the same all the way to Mexico and it was actually known by that name. This was almost entirely clear of obstruction and the homesteader who reached his location before dinner could 'turn the plough loose' as we said, and break up an acre or two before supper. This was the land of the 'bonanza' farms where according to the old legends the twelve- or twenty-horse plough teams went to the far end of the furrow and back and stopped for dinner then made another round trip and unhitched for the day. All this soil needed was water. In the old days the 'June rains' were a proverb, though somewhat less uniform and dependable in later years. A 'sloppy June' there — as everywhere in Alberta — meant almost invariably a good harvest since if the rains came at the right time they were not so likely to come at the wrong one. During many years I kept weather notes (without instruments) my general conclusions were that the annual precipitation was broadly equal, coming either as rain or snow; the real significance being when it came.

At its best the chocolate soil never raised as much as black soil could but there were never any doubts about it ripening. It grew a bright stiff straw that could stand any amount of wind without lodging in a region where the winds blew virtually every day. On a field in good heart wheat would stand virtually up to forty-eight inches in height. Up to that length the heads increase in length proportionately to the straw; beyond that no length makes any appreciable difference. You merely had more straw.

The true 'black soil' of the more northern scrub-and-timber lands produced and was produced by a totally different ecological cosmogony. The chocolate soil areas, while of course not literally free from herbage in amongst the grass, at a cursory glance certainly looked as if they were. On the other hand the blacksoil regions looked like an endlessly varied carpet of flowers, and were as varied as they looked. Professor John Macoun in the eighteen-seventies tabulated ninety-six grasses along with over a hundred other plants and flowers found within the long grass, black soil areas. In the same area, the black soil was attributed by some scientists to the ashes of the incessant prairie fires during many untold centuries. But this hypothesis overlooked the fact that in the drier and hotter southern territories where the Indian firings were equally

Breaking sod near Mound, Alberta, c. 1900

prevalent and no doubt fully as destructive, the soil was not black. The colour is now thought to be due more probably to biological-chemical influences.

The texture of the heavy black soil sod is much lighter than that of the chocolate soils, and if it were as free of roots as are the latter it would break up 'a horse easier'. It was so much softer than in the more wooded sections it was often found necessary to sink breaking ploughs to as much as six inches deep to give a hold on the 'landslide'. This carried the great advantage of going beneath the crowns of the willow roots and thus leaving nothing but the root suckers to be cut through. Since one might find these great roots anywhere on the surface, a sharp coulter was really more necessary than a sharp share. The big 'brush-breakers' had a very sharp chisel-point protruding in advance of the coulter and many a big root was pierced and torn out bodily that neither coulter nor share could ever have cut! The worst of all roots were the bushes about the height of a horse. The taller, older ones were frequently rotten at the centre and came away easily. Sometimes they lay so thick on the ground, that to clear them out of the way so that the disc harrows wouldn't merely be riding on wood without touching the soil, one had almost to hand-cultivate.

The orthodox time to break new land was June and early July. My own observations (based upon an 'unfortunate' year when I couldn't get there any sooner) led me to prefer not starting until mid-July if practicable. I had watched the plant life cycle. By mid-July the growth cycle for that year was past. The grass growths newly turned under rotted down there instead of growing through again as was general with the earlier breaking. These were very persistent, and almost turned the new ploughed land into a tough sod once more that only summer fallowing cured. I was led to this conclusion by comparing the earlier plots with the later ones in which the stubble was entirely free from grass-growth. The influence of the sun and rains of summer and the disintegrating frosts of winter produced apparent chemical effects which cultivation of the land broken at the wrong time utterly failed to achieve.

During the first two seasons with new land we almost prayed for a dry summer that would keep growth within manageable limits. Oats seven feet high and wheat sixty-five

31

inches were common. As I have explained, this extra growth brought no proportionate increase in yield. To prevent the extra handling of huge masses of butt-end straw with no more attraction to livestock than so many wire nails, we set the binders up to maximum height and left the stubble two feet long. This had the additional advantage of clearing any stray willow roots that might have been left on the land and could ruin a binder-sickle.

After 'backsetting' (second crop) the original sod had disintegrated thoroughly and the virgin herbage turned under was furnishing the maximum of plant food. Not from any 'scrap the plow' incentive of enriching the seed bed but for the deliberate purpose of retaining the seed in the event of an 'ideal', i.e., wet season, many good farmers would 'disc' in the second crop without ploughing. It was now that we longed for the power to foretell the season that we might sow accordingly. There were two main methods we could follow. One was to sow thinly and allow the plants to 'stool' freely. This permitted the plants to grow thicker and stiffer straw, rendering it less likely to 'lodge' if high winds came. Such a crop looked just as solid a wall of standing grain as any other and under suitable conditions could yield as much. On the other hand, each of the separate plants of which a field is composed had a materially larger area of rich soil from which to draw sustenance and unless a good period of hot dry weather intervened, they could keep on growing instead of ripening.

The alternative method was to sow more thickly. This gave each of the individual plants less proportionate space and facilitated ripening but the thinner straw resulting from this was much more likely to be blown over in a high wind. An exactly similar problem faced the farmer after summer fallowing.

The Dominion Experimental Farms seemed to me to rather 'miss the bus' in some of these dilemmas. Their reports contained abundance of details as to which of six or eight varieties of potatoes, turnips, carrots, beets, or onions had proved (fractionally) better in a given year but seldom offered any general advice about the particular varieties likely to pay best over a series of years in this or that type of soil. One often had also a wicked feeling of a super-breed of high priests who couldn't be touched with the feeling of our infirmities. These men were working without having to put down any stake on the board as we did. We used to say to one another that we'd like to give those fellows a dirty (i.e., weedy) farm to clean up — and make a living while they were doing it! We couldn't afford to be fallowing all the time.

There lived near us on the way to town a splendidly successful farmer, a youngish man from Ontario who I believe had never had any 'agricultural training' but had learned the business on the job. Though he never knew it, I made this man my own unofficial Experimental Farm. Everything he did was efficiently sound and in addition was well finished. His ploughmanship and his fences were the talk of the whole neighbourhood. In one huge field with no roots, and an abundance of horse-power, and by careful cross-measurement instead of the common haphazard 'pacing', he finished off his 'lands' so accurately that the final furrow, or the 'Dead furrow', required only the lowering of his plough to afford a side-grip, and the entire half-mile stretch was finished off in one unbroken and mathematical parallel. I never saw it done elsewhere. Due to the same abundance of horse-power, he was consequently well able to carry on his operations at the right time which in a land of short seasons was even more important than his meticulous excellence. A farming job well done when it's too late is *ipso facto* not well done.

He never let me down but once. No doubt for some good reason well known to himself, in clearing up the willow roots from a large field of new breaking, I noticed him hauling them off with a team and wagon. So I did the very same. From one eight-acre field I took off ninety wagon loads. Whether he had a materially large number too big to burn without more drying I never learned. But before I had another such task to face I did learn that with a very little coaxing the willow roots would burn up completely even that same fall with an enormous saving of labour and precious time in addition to the manuring from the potash. As harvest time drew near, the exact positions of the brush fires could be picked out a mile away from the further advanced condition of the colouring crop.

Years later, I discovered that the immense value of my friend the 'Experimental Farmer' to the working farmers of the province had attracted the attention of others besides myself. The University of Alberta conferred the Honorary Degree of

Master-Farmer upon Percy Switzer and another gentleman near Wetaskiwin (Alberta) considered equally worthy of the honour. The proposal caused a rather amusing *contretemps* in Faculty circles. The President at that time was a geologist. He took a dim view of the suggestion regarding the proposed honours. It was hardly the business of a university to dignify *farmers*! The President's relations with his Faculty heads were on a very tolerant basis, essentially that of *primus inter pares*; some of them were academically superior to himself. The Librarian was a member of four world-notable universities and another Head of a department was the author of the world classic on his especial subject. They reminded the chief that after all agriculture was Alberta's foremost industry. One hardy soul went further and 'carried the war into Africa'. He reminded the geologist that it wasn't really so very long since geologists themselves were held by the truly severe academics to be little more than helots-among-citzens, mere Gentiles in the Outer Courts whose admission depended very much upon the gracious sufferance of their betters. The opposition collapsed.

6

Social Frontiers

Everybody on the North American continent is familiar with the wide temperamental cleavage between the North and the South in the United States whether he has ever lived south of the Dixie Line or not. In Alberta obviously we had not the tremendous force of slavery acting as a separating force to keep us apart; neither was there that of any racial antipathy— even as between 'cousins' of the same stock. Yet the feeling of alienation was quite real and tangible.

The south regarded itself as the senior. They were the real 'old-timers'. From their own restricted standpoint this was true. But there were implications of social superiority also, quite independent of the mere accident of one's arrival in the country. Some of the early ranchers had come to the West originally as troopers in the very first Mounted Police force of 1873. Some members of this organization quite manifestly supposed their official advent to be the beginning of all things in the Canadian West previous to which era the earth was without form and void. They passed it on to the recruits of the 'second generation' that before their appearance no white men —certainly no mere missionary — dared to venture among the Blackfoot camps. Actually of course it was the 'spade work' and the character of the early missionaries since 1840 — Rundle, the McDougalls, and Father Lacombe — that rendered possible that trust in British law and justice which the first commander of the police, Colonel Macleod, so splendidly vindicated and engrafted in the Indian mind. It was the seed sown by those early evangelists that blossomed later in the single-handed exploits against hostile or doubtful Indians which are foolishly attributed to some vanished breed of superman. Individually the American soldier was often just as brave and just as tough, but an infamous 'century of

35

dishonour' frustrated his efforts. Faith in the white man had been killed.

Other ranchers well antedated the coming of the Canadian Pacific. Against this, northern Alberta had very few to show apart from the 'Hudson Bay bunch' around Edmonton and they were superciliously dismissed as "half of 'em breeds. . . ." Clearly then the south was the aristocracy; some of them were of the aristocratic caste in other lands before coming here. As Kipling puts it, they were quite definitely "we and everyone else was 'they'. . . ."

It is this peculiar attitude or sense which explains the southern response or reaction toward the later selection of Edmonton as the capital of the new province (1905) and the seat of the University of Alberta. It was very much as though a coloured candidate had been suggested for the presidency of the United States. It is perfectly certain that such a proposal would never reach the stage of an examination of cultural or educational qualifications. Until the firm determination of the Edmonton supporters came home to their minds and serious action was recognized to be necessary, the southern champions hardly dreamed of presenting Calgary's claims in terms of detail. Their response to the suggestion of a northern rival was a mere howl of derision from press and people at the bare mention. The obnoxious proposal was not opposed, criticized, or discussed as unjust, unwise, untimely, unworkable. It was merely denounced and dismissed as unthinkable. The case was laughed out of court.

This may perhaps partly explain their failure. They did not condescend to indicate factual objections or rival advantages until they had stung their northern antagonists by their open contempt. At this time of course, Calgary was unquestionably the real metropolis in actual fact. Edmonton possessed an historical continuity antedating her rival's by eighty or ninety years but that could be made a thing of naught. The same influences that had secured the removal of the old North-West territories capital from Battleford to the "main line" (i.e. of the Canadian Pacific, there was no other main line then) would without doubt be ready once again to intervene on behalf of Calgary's proud ambitions. But Edmonton also had now a powerful backer behind her. In the north had arisen a new pharaoh who knew not Joseph — or rather one who knew

Joseph altogether too well and Calgary's champions toiled and stormed in vain. Frank Oliver was too much for them.

One of the most extreme examples of this prejudice known to me came to our notice even before reaching Canada although we of course did not then recognize it for what it was. In the winter of 1891-1892 my parents met Dr. John McLean, the Indian missionary to the Bloods and Piegans of southern Alberta, in England. They told him of their desire to come to Canada, and of their intention to settle in the Red Deer district, as they subsequently did. This was his response: "What do you want to go into a wilderness like that for? Keep to southern Alberta!"

Dr. McLean was actually at this time a fellow member of the old North-West (Methodist) Conference with Dr. Leonard Gaetz, who was then demonstrating the high potentialities (and performances) of the Red Deer district itself. There was likewise another fellow member of the same body at this time who had come to the west about the time when McLean was born — Rev. Dr. John McDougall. McDougall, during thirty years of agricultural experience on the North Saskatchewan, had — like his father George McDougall years earlier — deliberately classified the northern territory as the cream of the Canadian West, which it actually is and had never at any time made any secret of his preferences. McLean was also cognizant — he could not have been ignorant — of the disastrous years in the yet unirrigated lands of the south. Yet thirty-five years later he could still write: "There was a prejudice against the open treeless country until Professor Macoun reported favourably of it. . . ."

There was also a tone, an atmosphere difficult to define but the presence of which was unmistakable. The southern point of view dominated the thinking of the territory very much as the landowning class dominated the thinking of the English countryside. It was in this subtle sense that the catchword mentioned above about "leaving the country same side up" gained vogue and became a sort of universal local postulate, even in the mouths of dissenters.

Southern Alberta, or at least the short-grass region, was the "stamping-ground" of the "cow-puncher." The northern lands (which term here signifies the North Saskatchewan territory) can scarcely be said to have furnished much material for romance since the passing of the exclusively fur-trading era. The colourful westerner of more modern times, certainly of more modern fiction, the personage who frequently arrogates to himself the title of 'Westerner' and is instinctively conceived as such, belonged to the southern country. His type-characteristcs are considered — in fiction at least — to embalm the west in capsule form.

Much fine writing has been expended on this genial, care-free, imperturbable soul, an unruffled spirit who never turns a hair in face of difficulty, danger, of disaster. But — if the bunch smothered in blizzards, or mired in quicksands, or drowned in high water, why should he worry! Like the similarly undisturbed railroad man whose engine is in the ditch and who will tell you (providing no one is hurt) that she isn't his, he doesn't own a single rivet in her; so the cowman owns nothing in the outfit but what he stands up in and his horse and saddle. He can afford to be easy. Let the old man do the worrying! Some of these men could "fly off the handle" fast enough where the possessions or their incidental griefs were their own. I knew one man of this type. He was not then actually a cowman but he boasted incessantly of having been one in several States and in speech, idiom and appearance he was the nearest personification of the stage Westerner in 'undress uniform' that I ever encountered. A giant of a man, six-feet-six and broad in proportion and never seen except in buckskins. I imagine his wife must have been absent or unwell or this hero would never have been milking the family cow (their only one). She kicked him; possibly a conclusive proof that animals can think! No cow was going to kick him! Nor did she ever kick him again. He took the shot-gun and killed her there and then. The Western equanimity must have been granted to the wrong sex in that home if the lady's later report is authentic: "He says — 'if we can't have butter we'll have beef an' we'd fried liver an' drunk the milk, both of 'em, for supper that same night!"

The cowman viewed the homesteader, nester, granger, sod-buster, with measureless contempt. He, who perhaps before bed-time might not even dare to call his horse and saddle his own if the evening game in the bunkhouse took a wrong slant, was utterly scornful of one who had to do his own worrying! Yet after three or four years the despised sod-buster, in spite of his appearance, probably possessed far more than most of the picturesque ineffectives would ever command for they were far enough as a rule from being as level-headed as John Ware, the well-known coloured ranchman, who worked his way up in course of time from man to master. With many of these and in a land above all lands supposedly without classes, the 'lower classes' beyond question were those who stood upon their feet as they worked! The daily avocations of the cowman were often sufficiently strenuous but so long as they were tackled in the saddle — that wasn't work; all other occupations of the out-o'-doors labourer were pilloried in the damning verdict "Too much like work!" The mental attitude of the type is crystallized in the familiar Western yarn of the fellow who quit because the boss wanted a well dug "an' it couldn't be done o' hossback!" Perhaps no dominant type has ever left so little permanent impression on a country or added so little to its lasting development. As a moulding force in the evolution of an Alberta civilization, they have been eclipsed by the sod-buster.

This self-elected aristocracy was without exception, culturally if not always geographically, of the South. Northern Alberta was the region whence came we poor down-and-outs who had left our poverty-stricken homesteads for a space in the urgent need of 'making a stake'. We drifted down in the summer to Calgary, the only labour market at that time, to work on the big hay camps or headed westward at other seasons for the Kootenay and the 'bush'. "Another goddamned homesteader, I guess!" Nobody asked where from. It was needless.

The essential physical and economic difference between the two great areas was recognized by the Territorial Government before the era of Alberta as a province in its own right. They enacted a herd law for the southern ranching country and a fence law for the northern farming districts. **Whatever the intention of these ordinances may have been, in practice they made the wealthy stock-owner virtually** independent in both territories. 'Herding' among the big southern ranchers was a dead letter. Their ranging cattle mixed promiscuously at large until the round-up. Any small farmer-owner on the border of the "cow country" was compelled both legally and perforce to herd his own milking cows if he wished either to bar them from his own or others' fields, which were not required to be fenced, or to keep them from straying away. While thus herding his own animals he was also engaged in herding those of wealthier owners — a task which legally devolved upon themselves — in endeavouring to restrain his own stock from absconding in the intruders' company. Conversely, in the fence law areas a well-to-do stockman could turn loose as many as he chose and for as long as he chose. Pasturage, haystacks, crop fields — these must be protected by those who owned them. The situation was not unlike that which was so corrosively satirized by the brilliant French critic, Anatole France. He poured scorn on the suggestion of 'one law for the rich and another for the poor'. "There was nothing to prevent a rich man, just as freely as a poor man, from sleeping under the dry arches of the Seine bridges of a winter's night just as often as he chose!"

Yet in relation to fires the law was made uniform over the entire North-West Territories and made from the standpoint of the ranching south exclusively. It was also administered very much in the same spirit. Little consideration was shown to most offenders. The plea of clearing land or even of burning brush which in the first instance had been cleared by other method than fire, was likely to meet with short shrift. Such a delinquent was much like a poacher before a bench of English county magistrates. It was really a rather striking demonstration of the status and efficacy of law as a reflection of public opinion. Public opinion — which in its vocal expression certainly appeared to emanate principally from the stockmen — was severe. Consequently the administration of the law was severe.

This is not purely an academic opinion. In the spring of 1896, I was myself arraigned in court on the charge of what was colloquially termed "putting out a fire" which in standard English would presumably mean extinguishing it. I believe the actual legal terminology was "allowing" a fire to run. As I recall that May morning, allowing scarcely seems the correct expression.

There was good reason to think that the informer in the case was a nearby neighbour, who had incurred no damage. Being legally under age, I was nineteen, with neither father nor guardian, "of previous good character," and having myself suffered the loss of every building excepting the home itself, I was bound over to keep the peace for six months which I succeeded in doing. A fellow-malefactor on this first occasion, who could only plead the third of my foregoing four "extenuating circumstances," and lost even that status before the close of the hearing, was fined twenty-five dollars and costs — a month's wages in those days — and for good measure was also severely lectured by the magistrate.

Fires, however, were too serious an occurrence in our lives, and — in my judgement at least — have been too serious an influence in the province at large, to be treated as a mere incident at the conclusion of any chapter. This entire incident will be detailed in a later section.

7

Pioneer Psychology

There were clear indications that a forest rearing and a forest environment, with its inevitable isolations and its close uniformity in everyday conditions of life, was a strong formative influence in the moulding of a definite character-type. In this connection, I do not now refer to the mere skill as a worker in the woods. That has been clearly crystallized in the familiar aphorism that "Canadians were born with an axe in their hands," and needs no further labouring. One of the chief of these 'forest' indications was a man who was not afraid of hard work. Sixty years ago mechanization in Canada was scarcely beyond its infancy for farm dwellers and the world of the man who felled his own timber to meet his needs was perhaps less affected by it than any other. But I have to say that I never encountered any vestige among these men of what may be termed a nostalgic inability to be content anywhere but in the wilds. Such a feeling was, I believe, much more common among the Old Country immigrants and particularly that overwhelming majority of us who had never owned a tree or an acre in our lives.

There is one vital factor in these imaginings which one may overlook or perhaps never realize. Not very often among pioneer settlers hewing their homes out of the woods, is the love of trees found to be a very active impulse. Even now, although temperamentally a tree-lover, in regard to the willow species I am too intolerant after years of warfare with them to **endure even an 'ornamental' weeping willow on my lawn. This** attitude is well described by one of the most penetrating students who ever analysed the pioneer psychology, Frederick Jackson Turner:

To the pioneer the forest was no friendly resource for posterity, no object of careful economy. He must wage a hand-to-hand war upon it, cutting and burning a little space to let the light in upon a dozen acres of hard-won soil, and year after year expanding the clearing into new woodlands against the stubborn resistance of primeval trunks and matted roots. He made war against the rank fertility of the soil. . . .

Turner was of course referring primarily to the American pioneer settler but the great forest territory of the Atlantic States and of Eastern Canada was geographically a continuous tract, interrupted only by the Great Lakes. His description of the mental reaction of the forest dwellers as an early type is authentic beyond question. The trees were the perpetual enemy, always with them and ready at the least pause of man's eternal vigilance to resume their ancient domain.

Turner's pronouncements find support from some curious historical facts drawn from earlier ages. The English have been called, and are, a "tree-loving people." Yet Dr. J. Charles Cox, an unsurpassed authority who had read enormously in the ancient royal Forest Records subsequent to the Norman Conquest, could find no reference of any character to a tree as a thing of beauty earlier than 1347. And this reference proves by its very nature that such a point of view was far from being common. Dr. G.G. Coulton, a scholar who was decidedly the foremost English mediaevalist of his time, cites corroborative evidence to show that even the two finest English poets of the same era, Piers Plowman the countryman and Geoffrey Chaucer the Londoner, were not unanimous on the question. I have heard occasional regretful allusions from friends, natives of the Eastern Canadian backwoods regions, concerning the enormous areas of magnificent hardwoods that had been destroyed by the settlers in clearing the land. It appeared, however, to be exclusively the economic aspect of the tragedy that was foremost in their minds. I have no doubt whatever that a twenty-acre field was an infinitely greater joy to the backwoods settler at the time than the forest he had swept away.

I was led to similar conclusions by careful scrutiny during some hundreds of miles of travel through 'Old Ontario', in regions I had never previously seen during half a century in Canada. I had been assured before-hand — and not by native Ontarians alone — that I should find these portions of that province beautiful to look upon. This was also my experience. Yet I could not avoid seeing that while almost all farms had their 'woodlot' which played an essential part in conferring that leafy diversity which is the glory of the English rural scene, it was quite commonly pushed away in a corner and was apparently an economic factor almost entirely. Some farms had a few trees near the home, many had none but the fields were almost invariably treeless. I have worked considerably with forest-bred Ontarians in the old days, men without exception of the 'homesteader' type. I cannot recall a single note of aesthetic regret at the clearing they or we were doing.

In one of my own fields, from which in order to throw two open areas into one, I had 'root-cut' and burned some forty sizable trees standing perhaps ten to the acre, there were three enormous white poplars growing out of one root. From a little distance they looked when in leaf like one of those huge, umbrageous field or hedge-row oaks which are designated in more than one English county "the weed of the shire." I am not sure that it was not their colossal size that spared them in the first instance. Later, however, it did occur to me that at some future time when fenced pastures had become the order of the day, they might furnish grateful shade to one's cattle in a broiling summer noontide.

It was actually an Ontario-bred neighbour who asked me why I had left them standing: "Too big for you, Frank?" This friend was far from being an extreme example of the Philistines. He was of a kindly and tolerant nature, a man universally respected. Perhaps even more noteworthy in the present connection — since leaving Ontario at twenty, he had spent nearly forty years in the States, principally in the treeless West, where they had many a time gasped in the blistering heat. Such a tree would then have been a phenomenon and a godsend.

Yet my explanation or 'defence' evoked no sympathy. My friend merely pointed out that a tree was a perpetual nuisance to steer implements around and that crops growing in the shade would never ripen properly and could scarcely even be cut. The argument, be it noted, was not of trees but of this tree since there was no other such growth, to tempt one to spare it, on the whole place. The 'loss of crop' (which in any event the cattle would eat after stacking or threshing was done) represented about one-fortieth of an acre! But my old friend was immovable. In travelling forty years later through the dairy lands of Wisconsin and Illinois, I was greatly attracted by the feature of the grand old trees left standing here and there in the meadows. Their generous shade must be a priceless boon to dairy cows in that land of scorching summers and a distinct economic gain perceptible even to the most sordidly 'practical' mind. Yet Ontario has a hot summer also, in close proximity to the same Great Lakes.

Even in Macoun's day the use of (horse-drawn) machinery on the farm had progressed far enough for the practical urge of the unbroken sweep across the field to exercise a subconscious economic influence in a farmer's mind. Whether this could have developed and triumphed so generally, over an aesthetic impulse of any appreciable degree of vitality, seems doubtful. For we may remember that the earlier generation of rural Ontarians were farmers; and not yet 'wheat-miners' caught up in the hectic whirlwind of the annual 'harvest rush'.

This narrowly, almost sordidly utilitarian viewpoint is forced upon the pioneer. What would be leisure periods in a later and easier stage of development must be, and commonly are, occupied with those minor but none the less necessary and insistent tasks which are thrust aside by the major demands of summer and winter days. For such reasons, however instinctive it may be to do so, it is misleading and unjust to draw invidious comparisons between the dweller in older lands who is seen tending his flowers in some trim little garden plot after his day's work and the pioneer homesteader whose similar 'leisure' task must always be something 'practical'. I am confirmed in these conclusions by what I have seen of the countless charming farm homes both in Eastern Canada and in the Central States and Middle West, which are peopled by the same essential type as the early homesteaders to say nothing of the modern homes in Alberta itself. At the present moment, however, our concern is neither to prefer indictment nor to offer defence but simply to notice the fact, however it came to be so, that the Ontario farmers in early Alberta were sternly practical utilitarians. Perhaps I should add before going further that 'Ontario' is not a mere prejudiced or slovenly synonym for 'Canadian'. I had been years in Canada before meeting my first Maritimer and during the whole of our farming years I never came to know one personally. Our Canadian neighbours were exclusively from Ontario.

The rural Ontarians were virtually without exception good farmers, certainly everyone among them who was well enough equipped to be able to demonstrate his capabilities in practice. Many were more than 'good', they were excellent. But to imagine them as a type being actuated by any form of aesthetic impulse — nostalgic or otherwise — or by any other incentive not purely practical, is exquisitely absurd. I have never known any instance of an Ontario farmer going farther back from his 'railroad base' than circumstances dictated, or taking a brush-and-forest farm from any sentimental longing for the environment he had left. I have certainly known such men to go farther back and take up a brush-and-parkland, or even a brush-and-forest farm, while more open land remained unoccupied nearer to a railroad but it was for what was known to be better soil, or where the place was nearer to heavier or better timber for building or fencing. But where both of such locations were free homestead lands, or were both selling at similar prices — in a word, where conditions were equal — I have never heard of such conduct.

In one instance a young and very energetic Ontario farmer sold out what had always been, even before he broke it up, a more than average open quarter-section and with the proceeds purchased a wild half-section on which the willow-scrub — not forest — stood so high and thick that "you could lose a man o' hossback on the place." But in this instance the farm he sold was fifteen miles from the station and the place he bought was less than four — no negligible item in the days when the farm motor-truck was yet undreamed of!

Directly across the road was another example, an old gentleman who was actually the very wealthiest individual working farmer settler I ever knew. This man bought outright a full section (640 acres) of Hudson's Bay Company land, of which one-half had neither tree nor bush on it; one of the only two tracts I ever saw in the northern country that was broken with a rolling coulter. This describes the place in a word to any experienced judge. He quite evidently preferred to buy within three miles of town, at a cost of two thousand dollars, than to go farther and have a fourth part of that acreage given him for nothing! This man also was from Ontario. In fact, the road-allowance on which these men dwelt was locally known as "Ontario Street," from this exclusive origin of its landowners for some six miles. It was not until this ancient capitalist sold out in due course that the first of the Gentiles from the outer courts gained admittance into the sanctuary.

We never had any direct intimation from these men, whom I knew very well, that aesthetic motives — if they could have been made to understand what such things meant — had exercised no influence in these transactions. One visible fact however was beyond dispute. No sooner had these men secured their respective properties than each of them stripped off the thickets of brushwood over their entire areas in readiness for breaking them up! Any supposed nostalgic longing got short shrift from its victims, tenants, custodians, or what you please to call them.

It is a risky matter to attempt to generalize, over a wide region, about the locations people choose to occupy. One potent influence in these selections should not be overlooked. I believe very few newcomers were left totally without guidance in a strange land, to choose a home-site purely on their unskilled native predilections and perhaps be very badly 'stung' in so doing. The Ontario homeseeker very frequently had former neighbours, relatives, or friends in the country. We had four 'colonies' in the Lacombe district. There were the London, Guelph, Leeds County, and Beeton 'clans' although in no single instance did these occupy a solid block of settlement having reached Alberta at different eras. There were also land guides available — and very necessary — for new arrivals from Britain or elsewhere who had no local acquaintance. In the case of the Old Country people in particular, who were unable to judge the soil beneath from the vegetation above (as an expert in this homespun ecology can do at a glance), such guides were really indispensable.

These land guides as a class were generally honest and reliable men. They had nothing in common with the 'slick' and frequently unscrupulous real estate operator in our cities, herding their victims out to see "the best buy in the city." They drew no commission, and had no axe to grind by recommending fraudulent propositions to unsuspecting strangers. They were not even 'professionals' in the sense of following that job exclusively. They were commonly the owners of local livery stables, charging the current rates per day. They obtained from the local Dominion Land Agent his current returns up to that date for the surrounding townships, in those directions from town offering a minimum distance from the railway together with the most suitable soil conditions, available timber, and the like. Such men are entitled to be judged by their fruits. I cannot recall a single instance of an immigrant from Britain who had come to the country to make a home by tilling the soil being found as a result of a land guide's advice, on one of those 'pleasing' or scenic locations which were utterly unsuitable for agricultural purposes.

To attempt to lump together under one designation as "Old Countrymen" three such completely diverse types as the British farmer or land worker, the artisan townsman, and the 'middle-class' quasi-aristocrat is merely preposterous. It by no means necessarily follows, either, that because a home-site is pleasing to the eye it must be a poor choice from the practical standpoint but the truth concerning such foolish generalization lies elsewhere. I actually have seen a number of such selections by Old Countrymen which truly enough were beauty spots and little more. In every instance without exception they were either the homes of wealthy ranchmen, where the practical requirements of the establishment were in other hands or they were the homes of the 'remittance man' type, who commonly aped the ranchman, and who had no intention of farming or of doing anything else which involved steady labour. For such individuals, the practical aspects of the case may be said to have no existence. They certainly had no significance. These personages modelled themselves in every practicable respect on their actually much wealthier rancher-countrymen. Their approach in this feature of the ensemble to such an extent as their finances admitted, was a most important item in the 'make-up'.

I suspect that this attitude of putting the picturesque foremost in one's estimates of a type or region of country may have been the explanation of one early historic judgement. General Robertson-Ross, the commander of the Canadian Militia (1876), considered the Porcupine Hills district to be the very finest locality he had seen in Western Canada. This is without doubt a region much superior to a wide extent of territory that had to be traversed in order to reach it. The soil is good and there is a more plentiful rainfall than on the dry plains areas in the south on either side of the Alberta-Saskatchewan boundary. It is not certain whether General Robertson had seen the Canadian West at large at that time or from just what standpoint beyond that of its personal appeal he was characterizing the locality. It is not probable that an absolutely unanimous choice of the "finest region" in Western Canada could ever be agreed upon. As a broad locality for homeseekers (prior to irrigation days) the relatively small area of the Porcupine Hills district would probably rule it out.

8

American Settlers

It is of course well known that large numbers of Alberta's early settlers came from the United States. To attempt to comprehend this immense host under the one simple designation of the "practical Yankee" would be entirely misleading. Absurdity reaches its climax in predicating a uniformity of conduct in such a mass, even had there been but the one type. Apart from any question of individual variations in temperament, from which no large aggregation of human beings is ever free, the American immigrants divided into two principal or major types. For our present purpose these may conveniently be defined as those coming respectively from the east and from the west of the Missouri River.

The first of these bore a considerable resemblance in general type-characteristics to excellent farmers of eastern Canada from whence a certain number of them hailed either in person or ancestrally. At the same time it would in my view be incorrect to suggest that such common traits were consciously derived from that source to any really substantial extent. Probably a similar backwoods environment had done much to evolve a broadly similar type. Like the Ontario farmers, these men (and their wives) were clean-living, careful, methodical, patient, painstaking, frugal, economical and they were hard workers. That final trait is one without which a man was and is out of place on a pioneer farm — or any farm today for that matter.

These people also possessed what may be termed a sense of permanence. Possibly the very fact in itself of their continued residence in that territory when the "call of the West" had sounded so irresistibly in countless ears, testified to something of the sort. Their 'fixed' improvements were put

50

down with something of the attitude of the older lands: it was as though their grandchildren might be living on the old place when they were gone. At the same time they were well abreast of the up-to-date adaptations and developments in their business of agriculture, and generally were fairly well equipped with what at that time were reckoned as its modern appliances. They exhibited also a good measure of that love of neatness and tidiness which many have found so notably characteristic of the farmsteads of Britain. They also (as a class) displayed a similar pride in the quality of the farm stock which they reared and drove.

In psychological characteristics, the resemblance to the Eastern Canadian country-dwellers was equally striking. This was an era when "annexation" was very much in the air on the southern side of the International Boundary. It was not by any means of the philosophical, "logically inevitable" order which was discussed by such men as Goldwin Smith. It was much more nakedly suggestive, not to say prophetic, of "coming and taking it." Canada, as a self-governing state in most essentials even then, was ignored. The talk was virtually all of it featured by a "twisting of the British lion's tail." We noticed that this invariably aroused our Canadians to fury; an attitude which was conspicuous in the response to the Conservative slogan in the Reciprocity election of 1911, "No truck nor trade with the Yankees!" Yet the two rural types were so closely alike that providing annexation was not mentioned, they "spoke the same language" and viewed life from the same angle, and got along admirably.

These general conclusions were formed years ago from abundant opportunities for observation at close range among near neighbours. So far as the external characteristics of the Americans are concerned, a summer journey some forty years later through the rural regions of Wisconsin, Illinois, and Iowa, over an area from which many of them had come, led me to conclude that my estimate was broadly sound and just. With regard to my foregoing suggestion on 'permanence', it was on this journey that I was attracted by the spectacle of the great shade trees in the meadows, to which I have alluded. Whether planted, or preserved from a general destruction of the virgin growth, they were clearly no striplings of yesterday. Somebody — and an abundance of 'somebodies' — must have had a vision of the future. Such things are obviously meant to be a heritage for posterity.

Most immigrants of this class came to Alberta in very favourable financial circumstances doubtless due in large measure to the rise in values in their own long well-settled territory. This had enabled them — quite probably tempted them — to sell out at figures which represented even more in a new land of free homesteads and relatively low purchase prices. It was a common opinion amongst us that a combination of Ontario and the Middle West resulted in a farmer type that would be hard to beat in Alberta.

The second of the two essentially American types I have mentioned were as fundamentally different from the foregoing as it is possible to conceive. They were the absolutely representative products and the exponents in actual practice of Frederick Jackson Turner's famous "Frontier Theory" of American civilization. They were the 'sundowners', 'hustlers', 'sooners', 'prairie schooner', covered wagon pioneers of the American West. In their own phrase, "where they hung up their hats was home." They soon made us acquainted with the characteristic qualities and defects of their kind. In both categories the results were plainly traceable in large measure to their environment. Their nature like the dyer's hand had become subdued to what it worked in.

They were good neighbours, open-handed and generous almost to a fault. I do not believe that anyone ever asked a meal or a lodging under their roof and was sent empty away. In a world where the few doctors we had were frequently unprocurable at need, and where the telephone, the Red Cross, the district hospital, or the district nurse had not even been dreamed of, no call ever came to them in vain. At any hour their women would leave home on an instant's notice to watch day and night by the bedside of some stricken neighbour in the crisis of disease or childbirth and bearing with them from their own scanty store what might perhaps be needful for those yet poorer than themselves. All this without a shred of expectation either of publicity or monetary reward.

These people were expert, resourceful, courageous, indomitable. What they didn't know about the initial stages of tackling a raw homestead proposition was not likely to be found out in a hurry by anybody else. They were the incurable

optimists who "trust on and think tomorrow will repay. ..."
And with all their sterling qualities of heart they were all too
likely to leave the world as little benefited and themselves as
poor as when they came into it. For they were of the tribe of
Reuben: "Unstable as water, thou shalt not excel. ..."

Precisely as there are mental constitutions with whom a
rather rustic shrewdness in abundant measure — which is all
such natures possess — has to serve in place of intelligence, so
also with these. Shrewdness, which is to wisdom very much as
the linguist is to the philologist or the musician to the
composer, had to serve them — very imperfectly — in place of
wisdom. They were shrewdness personified; wisdom seemed
to be beyond their grasp. They were innate gamblers; their
stake on the board was everything they had in the world. They
furnished the experience which made more cautious folk
decide not to go and do likewise. Was it not old Sam Johnson
who cynically defined second marriage as "the triumph of hope
over experience?" This class might be defined as the personification of hope over experience; sometimes triumphant,
sometimes disastrous but seldom "profitable for instruction"
— to themselves.

These men as a class had not the faintest vestige of that
prudent conservatism which leads a wise farmer to view his
acres as a heritage to be passed on to a successor. Yet they
knew no other life. They could "toil terribly" but only for the
immediate purpose of the moment and in their own way.
Every old homesteader in the scrub country is familiar with
those unsightly 'islands' which at first disfigured many a field
where a copse of mightier and heavier trees had stood.
Perhaps an acre or so in size, with a mass of stumps and
tangled rootage too heavy and too firm for any plough to tear
loose, an eyesore and a blemish in a well-tilled field, a weed
nursery and an unremunerative, annually-recurring nuisance
at seed-time and harvest. Neither the Old-Countryman nor the
forest-bred Canadian dreamed of leaving such a patch to mock
at him for very long. The one, who drew his ideas from the tidy
fields of Britain, could not conceive of such abominations
remaining unmolested. The other, personally or ancestrally,
had wrested all his acres by main force from such a jungle.
These men, after many years had passed, dislodged and
uprooted the enemy with team and chain and handspike, so

that plough and binder could follow their path unchecked, and the soil yield its fruit like any other. More often than not they drew more of a spiritual tonic from this final and crowning subjugation of the wild than the conventional breaking of ten easier acres could have brought.

Not so the Westerner, as he pre-eminently termed himself. He would be apathetically content to leave it there forever; at the very least — if he were still on the place in that era — until the plough could go through without undue resistance. There was no doubt something of method in his madness. Probably nobody knew better than himself that he would not remain there to be troubled with it very long!

In the old free-and-easy days of Western land regulations in the United States, when rival railroad routes were competing fiercely for development, a settler after "proving up" once could homestead over again in the same office, if land remained available in its district. It could be done almost endlessly in another county or in a neighbouring State either in person or under some convenient alias. Men took homestead after homestead in all too rapid succession. There were individuals personally known to me — some of them, like my old neighbour with whom I discussed my big tree, by no means the most extreme of their kind — who had repeated the performance eight or ten times. A bad season, two years in succession on some very exhausting crop on new land such as flax (the "two crops an' pull out" practitioners), a hearsay legend at fifth-hand of some new El Dorado flowing with milk and honey at which they caught like children agape for a miracle — the wind passed over them and they were gone and the place thereof knew them no more! Such men have been the ruin for years of countless farms and of whole districts.

I knew men personally who "pulled up stakes" in the spring for the Land of Promise seasoning their exit with corrosive characterization of the "goddamn location" they were leaving, and of the bunch of suckers and easy marks that didn't know no better than to stick in it! After trailing all round several western States through the summer, they returned in the fall to the derelict shack they had abandoned and in some pathetic instances to discover that a stranger had entered into their inheritance.

Even in the later years, when by reason of settlement having 'caught up' they had perforce become somewhat less nomadic, the innate old Adam was unchangeable. One thing these men would not do was to lift a finger to replenish their starving acres by any process that could not be effected behind a team. They were the true spiritual kindred of the cow-puncher aforementioned, who wanted to "dig the well o' hossback." Sometimes the manure-heaps grew to be so unmanageable that they rolled back into the barns "faster than you can throw 'em out again" and piled up in the sheds until a calf could scarcely stand erect without scraping his back on the roof-timbers. I have witnessed instances of such men abandoning their (log) stabling and hauling their house across to another site on the homestead rather than haul out the manure to their famishing fields. "When I gotta start packin' out dung (or a monosyllabic synonym) it's about time to be gittin' outa here!"

To one who has known this type both historically and personally it would be exquisitely comical if it were not almost tragical, to see such a type lumped together wth all other unspecified Americans as the crowning exemplars of the shrewd and the practical. Shrewd? No doubt, also some of the simplest and most gullible of mankind. Practical? Unquestionably, yet perhaps among the poorest judges the world has ever known of when their time and their labour were being wisely expended or merely thrown away.

The life must have possessed a definite attraction for certain dispositions of mind and these in their turn were moulded by its governing conditions. Two of the most typical 'Western Americans' I ever knew turned out on closer acquaintance to be town-bred Englishmen from Birmingham where certainly (not being gypsies) they could have had no opportunity to acquire or develop such affinities. They out-Heroded Herod by habit which had become second nature, in speech, personal appearance, and even in an almost conventional style in 'glad rags' for festive occasions, to which the breed were much addicted. They ran very true to form in another important particular. After one season in Alberta they 'headed back for the States'.

Circumstances made these people; changed circumstances, such as they had never before experienced, had now in some degree unmade them. With the filling-up of the 'last West' even they have had to settle down and 'stay put' somewhere. Spiritually they were no doubt — as numbers of them assuredly are lineally — the ancestors of the "wheat miners" of the present day. Yet from this truly ungenial soil sprang Abraham Lincoln.

I have always felt greatly drawn toward the figure of Lincoln's mother, in her noble, touching endeavours to implant in her boy something of desire of the good fruit of the Tree of Knowledge and something of reverence for the beauty of holiness. We may be quite sure — I am at least — that Nancy Hanks was not the only idealist of her class. Women, and above all the mothers, of the covered wagon led a hard life. Theirs was a veritable living sacrifice. In an age when Hollywood and Reno had not yet cast their blight over the land, these brave souls loyally followed their men, for richer or poorer, for better or worse, as they had vowed themselves to do. Yet in countless hearts there must often have risen a longing for a home they could call their own for something more than a day and a night and where they could see the fruits of their toil and rest amid the recompense of their hands.

Most of those who lived to see fifty were already old, far spent in a life which in theory should be one of the healthiest that humanity can live. And I have seen some faded and pathetic wisps and shadows of womankind who had yet some years to go to reach forty. They saved others; themselves they could not save.

9

The "Practical Yankee"

I attempted in the previous chapter to describe the "practical Yankee" (in his two fundamentally diverse types) as I knew him in the old days. In the present chapter the intention is to relate what he, or they, did. In this respect also the major portion of the canvas will be given, as it has already been given, to the Westerner since he furnished the bulk of the early Albertans who derived from the United States. The close general resemblance I have emphasized between the American from the older territories east of the Missouri and the settler from Ontario, renders a full-length particularization really superfluous in his case. In depicting the practices of the latter one essentially depicts the former also.

The reaction of the Western American to the potentialities of the Alberta of the turn of the century is lifted out of the realm of prediction by the march of time and out of the realm of probabilities, however convincing in appearance, by our knowledge of the event. What these men actually did is a matter both of common notoriety and also of historical record.

Whatever the practical Yankee (as the botanist Macoun called him) might have 'known' about the 'baldheaded prairie' being the best location for him to settle on, cold facts tell a different story altogether. The precise type of Americans whose knowledge of the open plains territory of the West was the widest, that is to say the 'prairie schooner' class I have been discussing, actually crossed two hundred and fifty miles or more of that exact character of open territory from the International Boundary northward for the purpose of seeking a home in the allegedly 'inferior' northern scrublands.

In making this choice there were important factors quite

57

irrespective of any questions of soil or its freedom from brush — the governing factor, both for the covered wagon immigrant and the poorer ones (such as ourselves) from other lands, was the economic one. It is quite true in the abstract to say that the practical Yankee recognized this. Sooner or later most men do who are unable to defy its restraints. But the true governing economic factor was not a mere matter of somewhat easier or harder conditions in breaking up the virgin sod. The prairie schooner immigrant was a poor man in worldly goods and chattels, however rich he might be in dearly bought experience. A team and possibly two or three spare horses if he were so fortunate as to have such and a boy or two to ride or drive them, a breaking-plough, by no means always a stove, and a few of the absolutely indispensable tools and household utensils, together with some provisions for the trail (hopefully renewable at intervals), very commonly comprised his entire possessions. His wealthier Middle west countryman could bring a carload of effects. This would include dairy cows and heavy implements. These things were both too heavy and too bulky for covered wagons where the meagre space was at a premium. What was such a man to do with his scanty resources on the treeless plains of what was to him a northern land?

There was a further phase of the economic factor in the southern country. In the eighteen-nineties almost the entire territory from the International Boundary to Calgary and northward practically to the scrub country, was already occupied by ranchers. Virtually the only farming sections were the Springbank settlement between the Bow and the Elbow rivers, and a thin fringe along the Macleod Trail for a few miles south of Calgary.

It did not take an experienced freighter very long to recognize a ranching country when he saw one. Ottawa was making the most determined efforts, about 1894, to insist that "in spite o' hell an' high water" (or rather, no water) southern Alberta was really an ideal farming region. One must suppose that the C.P.R. which was then popularly defined as being "the Government" was favourable to this. Otherwise the campaign would probably not have been carried on. For similar reasons, although I have no definite knowledge, it is probable that the southern area, or much of it, was surveyed in sections on the homestead basis. I do know that this was the case with the northern open plains territory beyond Calgary. In all probability the practical Yankee was fully entitled legally to take a homestead almost anywhere. But these attractions cried aloud in vain. A deserted shack with its blown out field proclaimed the truth too clearly for such a trained observer to mistake.

There were also the men already on the ground to think about. Cattlemen in the West have never been very tolerant of any intruders of other classes. Their attitude toward sheep ranching is crystallized in a well-known Western yarn, which has been told of many regions and could be true of most. The newly-arrived parson had invited "the boys" at the conclusion of the cattle drive to attend church and the gang responded in force. The parson delivered an eloquent discourse on the Tenth Chapter of the Gospel of John following upon which the plate went around, to which they contributed liberally. Before the meeting dispersed the foreman of the "Lazy Y" requested permission to "say a few words" which the delighted preacher readily granted. "Parson, we've let you say your say this mornin', an' you can't say we didn't chip in like square shooters when the hat went around. We aint agoin' to hold it agin' you what you said this mornin', because you're green in these parts an' you gotta lotta things to learn. But this is a cow country. Get that! If we're comin' back next year we don't wanta be hearin' nothin about no 'good Shepherd'; becos there aint no such a thing! I never seen one yet. . . . "

An approach of this tone was not likely to be softened toward the "sod-buster" who was alone and unsupported in the face of powerful foes. The common cow-country methods of active repression were quite familiar throughout the West. Over the Boundary custom triumphed over law, or more frequently custom was law. It generally took some little time to convince a Western American that law prevailed over custom in Canada. He figured that a homesteader who owned little more than what he stood up in could not speak with the enemy in the gate to much purpose, and might look for a "rough ride." The Southern territory was summed up very succinctly: "That aint no sort o' country for a poor man!" Quite apart from any social considerations, it certainly was not. In addition to those items which had to be bought anywhere whatever the type of country, such matters as fencing, fuel, and most probably buildings were none of them very readily available from the natural resources of the region.

The northern scrub-and-forest area was radically different. It was the natural region of the homesteader. There was timber in abundance. This was very fair quality for building, and excellent for fuel and fencing. Almost equally important, it furnished shelter. This last factor enabled poor people to live in fairly comfortable conditions without those finished conveniences in details of home equipment which only money can supply and which so many modern "gadgeteers" conceive as elementary necessities. The days of central heating were not yet. But nobody who has lived in the same type of log (or other) home will dispute the wide difference in everyday winter comfort between the open prairie and the woods. I am speaking from experience of both situations.

The same regions seemed to provide shelter in quite another sense, a psychological one. They were a kindly veil behind which such relative or positive poverty as existed between man and man could hide its occasional shame from sight until the dawning of that better day toward which we unconquerably or incorrigibly looked. If Latin America is the land of "tomorrow" (mañana), our West was — as it still is — the land of "next year." As in most societies, there were those among us who had either enjoyed a better start, or had made a more skillful or more fortunate use of what they had. Yet the poorer ones, among whom the present writer is to be numbered, were seldom oppressed, and never to their faces, with the proud man's contumely. There was in general a broad and genial camaraderie which prevented the richer from parading their better fortune or the poorer from envying it in any cankering bitterness of heart. At times no doubt we should have liked a little more but in all probability "next year" would remedy that.

It was possible for a poor man who possessed little more than his two hands to at least grow much of his essential food supply. The man who owned a team and a couple of cows, together with the more elementary farm implements, could look almost anyone in the face. Though seldom as rapidly as they expected, from such a modest beginning many became well-to-do at any rate in the relative interpretation which the term connoted amongst ourselves.

To imagine that the foregoing attractions or alleviations which the scrub country offered to the poorer settler would be outweighed in the mind of the Western American by the enormous labour involved in clearing with bill-hook and brush-scythe is a ludicrous error. It is also an error which reveals its proponent's real ignorance of the type. The Ontario man and the English immigrant might prefer to clear off their jungle of brushwood green, "the hard way." Both of these frequently entertained a constitutional dread of fire. Very probably in the first of these this arose out of earlier experiences either personal or traditional. In the second it was quite as probably a timidity resulting from sheer inexperience perhaps reinforced by that subconscious preference I have mentioned for the "Canadian way" of doing things. Possibly too their conservationist unwillingness in both men to destroy a rich bed of plant food on the soil surface, into which in the scrublands one could plunge his hand well nigh to the wrist. And immigrants from Britain, whether rural or urban, had been familiarized all their lives with the constant necessity for manuring.

The Westerner cared for none of these things. If he could find a reasonably open patch for his first year's breaking, fire could provide for next year's "brushing." It was a thing of no importance if it did destroy some few thousand tons of inestimable plant food and vegetable humus classified in his vocabulary as "rubbish" or "old bottom." I have alluded to his aversion for jobs that couldn't be done behind a team. Six months or so after burning, the brittle sun-dried stems of the willow could be broken off short at the surface of the ground by some such appliance as a very heavy log. This was drawn transversely across the land by a team on each end. One super-resourceful individual even improved on that so I was told by one of the tribe. He abstracted by night one of the "spare rails" which railway companies keep in readiness at every milepost for unforeseen emergencies. One or two further holocausts, with a proportionate destruction of more plant food and the entire place would be cleared without even the necessity for raking up the debris with a hay-rake — "while them other back numbers is thinkin' about the business!" A scrub location had no terrors for such devotees and exponents of direct action.

10

Remittance Men

The remittance man in the days of his glory was distinctly a phase of the older society. The race may not be extinct, since it is dangerous to predicate the final disappearance of anything. Yet I doubt whether they can be as picturesque as of yore, any more than is the old Plains territory which was once their chosen stamping-ground.

Their principal function there was to bring Englishmen into disrepute. In this they achieved an abounding success. Yet they were often sinned against as well as sinning. Frequently they may have deserved sympathy quite as much as blame.

The general externals of the type are fairly well known. It was a kind of superstition-cliche that the remittance men were commonly, or at least often, parson's sons. Statistics have exploded this illusion; but they haven't necessarily silenced the croakers on the subject. Perhaps the offences of the parson's son seem more conspicuous. Certainly, among my own rather varied personal acquaintance of this breed, the parsons' sons were by no means the worst.

I well remember two partners. Both were from well connected families, or what were claimed to be such by their local representatives. The father of one was, at some time, mayor of the English railway town of Crewe. The other was the son of a distinguished officer in the Indian Army; a contemporary of such men as Lawrence, Havelock, and John Nicholson. These two men had sunk to an unimaginable depth of squalor and filth, physical and moral. I once had dinner in their shack (off tin plates) at the aristocratic hour of six in the evening. The shack itself was a heterogeneous assemblage of fragments of scrap or stolen lumber nailed together anyhow, roofed with a crazy pattern work of shingles, sections of tar paper and kerosene tins hammered flat, and of no describable design beyond a resemblance to a huge square packing-case dumped on the prairie. Truly indeed a thing of shreds and patches! How it kept out the weather — if it ever did — remains a mystery.

Inside, it was dismal beyond words. It appeared never to have been swept since Adam was a boy. The two inmates were extensive patrons of a certain establishment up Nose Creek. They defrayed the not-inconsiderable expenses of these recreations by hauling the winter's coal for the regular resident staff from the Knee Hill mines sixty miles away.

Another whom I knew was holder of one of the original baronetcies of the earliest King James I creation, and of a knighthood a century older than that handed down from his direct ancestor, a counsellor and executor of Henry the Eighth. This personage had been an officer in the original North-West Mounted Police and in this capacity had rendered distinguished service in the tragic interregnum between the final disappearance of the buffalo and the inauguration of regular provision for the Indian tribes. He had "gone squaw man," as Westernism has it, and had lived for many years with an Indian woman in the most abject condition. The contrast between his general (and irretrievable) appearance after such a life, and the clear-cut cultured speech which he had still retained, told their own tale of a grievous decline and fall, before one knew anything of the actual facts. I myself only learned much of these after his death.

The Dominion Land Agent at Red Deer in those days, the man who "inducted" my father and three years later, myself, into our respective homesteads was one of this type, who had by this time grown old, like Falstaff. Incidentally, he was a "townie" of my own, a scion of one of the great Sheffield steel firms whose names were household words in many lands besides their own. In his particular case, the name was still unchanged on their huge plant when I passed that way in 1948.

The fascinations of making steel in black, industrial Sheffield had piped unto him, but he had not danced. In 1894 he had already been in Western Canada, after much wandering, for many years. His way of life had fallen into the sere, the yellow leaf; like Dickens' Mr. Snevellicci it was a

63

wavering between intoxication partial and intoxication complete. His official formula, according to scandalous report, ran thus; "Take the book in your right hand and swear that this your affidavit is the truth the whole truth and nothing but the truth so help you God twenty-five cents come and have a drink. . . . " I can only suppose that my own homestead entry occasion must have been on one of the lesser days. Perhaps my extreme youth — I was at the minimum age limit — or the recollection of my father, whom he remembered having died in Red Deer during the intervening three years, may have swayed him. I was treated to a fatherly exordium on my status as a potential landed proprietor, seasoned with a repetitive refrain on Bulwer Lytton's "What will he do with it?"

Where the new recruit was thought to be old enough to take care of himself, this ancient toper was more of a pacemaker than any sort of counsellor. Twenty miles away we heard of the evil fame of a drinking gang in Red Deer, of which he was a prominent ornament. One young fellow whom I knew slightly literally drank himself to death, and had suffered the horrors of *delirium tremens* long before the end. What made this tragedy particularly poignant was the fact that his parents were the two outstanding members of the British peerage who were among the leading crusaders in the Total Abstinence movement.

As a type, the remittance men seemed to fall into very familiar lines of classification. In many particulars, when you had seen one you'd seen them all. But not completely so. Perhaps a basic line of demarcation would be between the drifting incompetent and the positive rotter.

Although in many cases anything but the most docile old horse was beyond their skill, nothing less in saddlery than a sixty-pound Cheyenne steel tree was worthy of their patronage. They were seldom seen, and never in the public eye, without the full regalia of the range. A swimming party was the only occasion on which one could be sure of catching them without their "chaps"; to hope to do so in bed was considered dubious. I have known such fellows on occasions when it was unavoidable to drive to town with a wagon, to park the abomination somewhere on the outskirts away from any house; and to walk up-street in the orthodox insignia of Stetson, chaps, and voluminous handkerchief to camouflage the degrading contamination of wheels and harness.

No doubt the parents of these pretenders meant well, in that loose idle sense in which probably nobody but an Iago or a Quilp has ever meant ill since time began. But such vague intentions, compared with the manner in which they were put into effect, remind one of Dickens' pious hope that his son might not grow up into a snob, while at the same time selecting Eton for the young gentleman's education as the best possible preventive.

Within the flexible limits of a lower middle-class environment, they were brought up to expect virtually everything that was going. After an education within the sheltered sanctities of the English public school system — sometimes onward to the university — they were suddenly confronted with a staggering ultimatum. "This night shall thy soul be required of thee!" The hitherto indulgent parent, who often had trained them by heredity and example in the importance of having a good time, had now other plans in view. He wanted them to put their noses to the grindstone in some avocation for which their native tastes and their whole life previously had cultivated a complete incapacity or a positive nausea.

Perhaps, by way of variety, the intimation would be that he could no longer afford to keep them around doing nothing; they must strike out for themselves. I have known several of this character who rebelled at being thrust as square pegs into round holes; and who were technically not remittance men only because "the old man couldn't or wouldn't send the remittance."

Sometimes they came as premium-paying farm or ranch pupils. One occasionally heard critical neighbours censuring so-and-so for "not even pretending to teach those fellows anything. . . ." It wasn't easy. Most of them had no desire to learn anything that couldn't be acquired in the barroom on Main Street. The occasional exceptions, who might feel a twinge of conscience over "the old man at home" were a constant headache. They had to be watched incessantly.

It was almost impossible to send them out on any serious undertaking without a smash. Sometimes the horses reached home on the dead gallop and nobody knew whether or not the fellow's neck was broken until he came limping in hours later. They couldn't hold a plough or drive a sulky plough straight. They turned harrows over on the horses' backs. They were likely as not to get down in front of a hay-rake or disc with the lines on the ground and have the team bolt over their bodies. No man dared trust them with a dangerous geared machine such as a mower, and few cared to leave a sharp axe within their reach. On the whole it was fortunate for all concerned that they commonly disdained these occupations. The very name of "farmer" was a thing of scorn. A local gag concerned one of these greenhorns who was proving up on his homestead. "How many acres broken?" inquired the land agent. "What do you suppose I am? I'm not a blahsted sod-buster; I'm a rancher." "Well, in that case, what stock have you got on the place?" "We-ell, there's the cayuse . . . and there's the dog. . . ."

Others whom I knew were rotters as well as misfits. Our camp cook at the Chipman Ranche in 1902 was a specimen. Even here, however, one has to be fair. If I had to choose between facing the Recording Angel in the role of Buck or Buck's father, I believe I should feel easier in the first one. Buck had been premium apprentice to a great engineering and implement firm in Lincolnshire where drunkenness and absenteeism had comprised his record. Except for the premium he probably would not have lasted his first month. That peculiar optimism which credits a new land with miraculous power to rebuild such a character by some force of its own impelled his people to ship him to Alberta. I had the particulars from Buck's own lips.

He was given £2,000 ($10,000) cash, with an additional solation of £50 per quarter for running expenses and pocket money. The lad apparently came west with some intention to play the game but if it is possible to conceive a newcomer who was greener than anybody else on earth, surely it must have been Buck. After making a dicker for the purchase of a ranch, Buck asked the vendor, "And now, what do you value the buildings and improvements at?" I quote the vendor's own words after the deal was completed: "When I heard this Englishman say that, I was just goin' to holler 'Well of all the damned fools!' Then I seen all at once who'd be the damned fool an' I shut my trap just in time! An' that simp paid me over again for the fixins."

Such a transaction obviously reduced the amount available for stock, and by the time Buck had engaged a foreman there wasn't much left of the £2,000. Still the quarterly £50 helped a little and for about three years Buck was the king of good fellows. In a very short time, between mysterious diseases in Buck's livestock (supposedly traceable to moving accidents by flood and field) and not at all mysterious increases in the arrears of wages owing to his accommodating foreman, the latter's equity in the enterprise exceeded that of the nominal proprietor. The business changed hands *de jure* as well as *de facto*.

Buck took on the job of camp cook, which was one greatly favoured by what may be termed ex-remittance men. I was never informed why but there seemed to be an impression that it was easier and "not so much like work." Truly enough the cook and his assistant were off in the broiling summer afternoons while the rest of us worked. But they worked earlier and later when we were off. I have often thought that it enabled them to keep to themselves rather more; and I know that most of them prepared themselves private menus more recherche than ours. In Buck's case, however, he was lame, so it was very much a matter of Hobson's choice.

Buck, of course, wasn't the first remittance man who had "come a cropper" in the ranching game. For the purpose of insuring a continuance of the regular remittance, the species pooled their information very much as the detective forces of the world are said to do. By these methods they developed quite a scientific technique for "putting it over the old man." There were still a number of wealthier or more conventionally minded individuals who kept up their wardrobes of "soup-and-fish" clothes, and even dressed for dinner more or less regularly, as they are said to in East Africa. There were others who required such trappings occasionally as lodge regalia, etc.

It has been known for a bunch of impecunious lads to borrow, or even hire such garments for an evening ostensibly "in memory of old times," or sometimes for the openly avowed purpose to which they were afterwards put. More than one of the down-and-out fraternity had such assemblages photographed, and the productions were sent home to the old man — "a few friends I entertained at the ranche recently."

Buck staged another variation of the camouflage theme. In his good cause the photographer snapped a bunch of range cattle, pedigreed bulls, ranch buildings, cowhands, and all the trimmings. They belonged to somebody else, but one can't have everything. Buck's father lived in Sao Paulo, Brazil. He was naturally gratified that the young scapegrace, after all he'd cost, was making good at last! The quarterly £50 still came with appreciated regularity. Now, in addition, came a handsome little cheque toward the cost of meeting the family in London for an English vacation. Buck reached London with three cents. "I wasn't going home with that! There was just enough for half a pint. When I rang the bell at my cousin's in Kensington, I hadn't a dashed cent on me!" I think the official explanation was that he'd been robbed on the boat coming over.

Before long Buck returned to Alberta, where he quickly went back to his normal existence: three days in paradise, three months in purgatory. Some time later, the outfit to which he was attached was driven into Fort Macleod from some routine job to be paid off. Buck gravitated to his natural orbit to the hotel where the barkeeper warned him to "get into the clear while the gettin's good. There's an old guy been stickin' around for two or three days askin' for you; an' if he ain't your old man I am! They told him you'd likely be in this week-end, so he reckoned he'd stick around."

Buck agreed concerning the wisdom of immediate action; but before he could act the door opened and the old man walked in. Perhaps Buck himself will tell the tale best, as he did to me:

"Well! I didn't know I'd such an expert liar for a son before. You can do that, if you're good at nothing else! I had to step up to New York on business, so I thought I might as well come on here and look you up. I've been here three days and I know all about your grand herd of other men's cattle and all the rest of it. Now I don't want to hear another word from you. But I'll tell you what I'm going to do.

"If you'd like to come back to England with me and attend to business, we'll forget all about this and let bygones be bygones. But I want a straight deal from now on. If not, you'll get no more money out of me; not a penny! And you can go to the devil in your own way."

Buck wound up with the following observation "I suppose I was a damn fool. I told the old man to go to you know where; and I haven't heard from any of 'em since."

Buck told me all the foregoing purely as an objective

recital of facts, a mere summoning up remembrance of things past. The sole suggestion of anything like remorse or regret was in the conclusion I have mentioned.

There is little more to tell. The Chipman hay camp outfit, in 1902, were paid off in Calgary on the Saturday night and in the absence of any Sunday train north I was held in town over the weekend. Calgary in 1902 had not yet outgrown the small town diversion of going down to meet the train and this year, with the inauguration of the *Imperial Limited,* Calgary was revelling in the luxury of a coast-to-coast flyer passing through in daylight.

On this occasion apparently everybody who was anybody in Calgary was there on the platform. Among the citizenry was Buck; and such a Buck. He was dressed in an English gentleman's outdoor rig of a rather sporting type, impeccable to the last detail; and he was limping up and down the platform in the very forefront of the crowd. He might have been an English country squire, British M.P., Foreign Office diplomat, or anything you please waiting to take the flyer. At that moment, twenty-four hours after pay day, he possibly owned what he stood up in, and nothing more.

Alas, poor Buck, so representative of his class, has probably long since joined the great silent majority. Yet in spite of all his failings, and they were not few, he and his fellow remittance men added a vivid touch of colour to the story of the West, which should not be forgotten. Through a mist of mingled laughter and tears shines the brightness of their memory.

11

Sport and Subsistence

It would be misleading to suggest that even in that distant era, wildlife either for sport or subsistence, played any very important part in our daily lives. Thirty years before our time Lord Milton and his companion Dr. Cheadle wrote (1863): "The days when it was possible to live by the gun and net alone have already gone by on the North Saskatchewan..." Although a considerable amount of "living by the gun" was actually being done in regions farther north and westward from us, it is still true to say that in 1894 the larger wild game was not really plentiful in the more settled areas. It had to be looked for, and sometimes one could look long.

This does not mean, however, that there was literally none. As an Albertan of two or three weeks' standing, I well remember riding home one evening on a load of hay. My brother and a farmer host were facing forward and I was looking back. I called to the driver to wait for a moment while his two colts, which had been following their mothers around the hayfield all day, caught up with the team. He at once said they were alongside, and had been throughout. Looking back on hearing this, the elders recognized the "colts" as two does of similar size and colouring following us home. In our second winter, 1895-1896, a trapper named Cummings (of whom I know nothing further) had a shack in the Red Deer Canyon. This was about five miles from us, and perhaps seven miles directly south from Lacombe at which place that precise portion of the canyon is visible from the train. I never heard any closely itemized description of his winter's take; the account at the time was that he had bagged eleven bear and smaller game in proportion. Judging from fur returns at large, this would mean much greater numbers of the latter class.

The winter following, 1896-1897, should have been a much better trapper's winter. It was intensely cold throughout with continuous and very deep snow thus making for easier tracking of animals and a high quality of fur. I never heard specifically whether Cummings' trapping range was trapped out or not. Certainly neither he nor any successor occupied the shack that winter. I know this to be true for a chum and myself spent a night in the shack in the height of the trapping season in February. It was entirely deserted and had manifestly not been used that winter. During our overnight stay in the canyon we neither heard nor saw anything in the least suggestive of the previous year's plenty. We found a gloomy, silent world.

It did not occur to us at the time since we knew nothing of the subject but this was the cyclic year of the periodic rabbit disease. If we had known of this visitation, we might probably have been more hesitant about taking our horses down there, since we had to blanket them outdoors in the warm, windless canyon woods for the night, there being no room in the tiny shack six by six feet square. The rabbit mortality had probably then been raging — or had raged — to its logical conclusion since November. Consequently the disappearance of animal life was most likely neither a local extermination of fur bearing species nor a progressive backward shrinking of the 'fur frontier' but a mortality or a migration of the predatory creatures, following upon the extermination of the rabbit population which constituted so much of their food.

The same occurrence may have had something to do with an apparently permanent reduction in the coyote numbers. During our first winter, 1894-1895, we heard a great deal about poisoning coyotes. Among the experts the approved method was to pour strychnine into hot melted fat which was then allowed to freeze. Unlike lean, it could thus be bolted whole without chewing, melting again in the stomach before the taste could be detected. The procedure required great care but numbers were actually caught by this trick. Perhaps the principal indication of a reduction in numbers was in the rarity, or absence, of local allusion to the poisoning industry after our first two winters. Here again it may have been the positive reduction of the parent stocks by poisoning or once more the reaction from the rabbit mortality. As in so many analogous situations throughout the world, the men on the ground in the crucial years were either ignorant or uninterested. In our immediate vicinity, speaking broadly, the coyotes (which were never really numerous) and their winter tracks appeared to be much the same throughout our time there as they were at the beginning. The three which followed my mother home were the most we ever saw together in our locality though I once saw seven at once on the plains south of Calgary and my mother's three were as late as 1905. I have heard the timber wolf of a winter night while hauling coal up the Red Deer River and have seen furtive shapes along the banks but never by day to be certain.

The coyote was a most cunning creature. I have known them to pass within easy range with insolent disdain, scorning to be hurried, when one had no gun. When we had, what was probably the same animal — being seen in the same spot the following day — would keep hopelessly out of reach. And how could a creature which had in all probability never been shot at, associate the smell of powder with danger?

As in the case of the two does mentioned at the beginning of this chapter, various game animals were occasionally seen in accidental circumstances. A bear and two cubs were seen near Alix, six miles west of Buffalo Lake in 1921. This was in a region which had been occupied since 1888 by a hunting community which included such doughty sportsmen as the Parlbys, Rowe and Westhead, Billy Bullock, the Haynes family, Matthew Cook, and the Bremner family around the Tail Creek settlement. In the city of Edmonton, one Sunday morning in 1930, about breakfast time when many citizens were sleeping in, I saw a handsome full grown doe on the corner of 101st Street and 118th (Alberta) Avenue. But even in 1894 our local hunting fraternity had commonly to go farther afield toward the Tail Creek and Buffalo Lake country heading toward the Hand Hills and the Plains. They seldom returned quite empty handed.

In this connection, I am reminded of a rather amusing episode at our first Christmas dinner. The oldest settler in the area east of the Edmonton Trail was old Isaac Haynes. Haynes station on the Rocky Mountain House branch of the Canadian National, which runs over my mother's homestead, was named after him. Haynes lived in the precise direction I have indicated above; the common cliche was that "the next house was at Moose Jaw" (some 450 miles away). Old Ike's son George came alone a week or two before Christmas with a most attractive haunch of venison which my father bought and which duly appeared on the board on the great day.

One of our three guests was an elderly Scot; the one who congratulated my mother on the dinner "so royally served." Scotty Walker (who was popularly computed at some two hundred years of age, since nobody could have achieved his varied exploits in less time) had without doubt seen a good deal of the world. He was an authority on everything and was dominated by a ruling passion for wanting to be the first to pronounce judgement perhaps lest it be thought that he was merely echoing somebody else. As the *piece de resistance* course terminated, Scotty leaned back in his chair in the manner of a finished connoisseur: "Well, Mrs. Roe, I canna' call to mind when I've tasted a finer bit o' beef in my life!" . . . "Thank you, Mr. Walker, But it wasn't beef, it was venison." . . . "Come noo, Mrs. Roe! Ye canna' tell me yon was venison. Ah've tasted too much venison in my time for that!" (rushing on his fate). My parents' firm insistence that it was truly venison, buttressed by readily verifiable particulars of its purchase from George Haynes, must finally have shaken him for crass assurance gave place to doubt; "Well! Ah never would have thought. . . ."

At a much earlier stage in the discussion, however, the data in the case had convinced his two delighted chums. They had been familiarized *ad nauseam* with a Scotty who in the Hielands could no doubt have told that deer's pedigree and what particular laird's forest it came from, from a single perfunctory sniff as it came to table. I heard fragmentary snatches of their infuriating goadings for weeks after: "It wouldn't have been so bad if you'd said 'mutton', Scotty; but beef. . . ."

I was out in the woods on one occasion with a bachelor friend — which signifies not merely an unmarried man but one who was 'batching' in his own shack by himself. It was in the early spring with the snow not yet entirely gone. We came across a big doe lying dead in the woods. We concluded that she had been shot, with a wound not immediately mortal, and had been able to get away from the hunter but had eventually perished from loss of blood. The body had been buried in deep snow throughout a cold winter; it was also drained of blood and to all appearance perfectly fresh. I don't know how we stood with respect to the law in such matters but my friend who was none too well off for fresh meat determined to take it home and try it. Between us, by a judicious adherence to certain "bypaths and indirect crook'd ways" known to few beyond ourselves in a woodland terrain, we got it safely home unobserved, and ate of it later more than once. Beyond being rather dry — not unusual with venison — it seemed perfectly all right and caused no trouble.

It is supposed to be the correct thing among many self-styled epicures, to greet moose meat with rapturous paeans such as no mere stall-fed oxen must ever call forth. I have never been able to agree to this. I admit readily that had I been mushing along all day behind a dog train in forty below, a big chunk of moose meat (or perhaps far worse) would no doubt be highly acceptable. But to sit down to a table and speak of preferring it, impregnated with spruce twigs, before beef, is beyond my comprehension. "Of course, it's got to be properly cooked!" say the rhapsodists. So be it. Properly cook the beef also; I still know which I should always prefer.

With the exception of the rabbits, our main shooting was among the prairie chickens, or more briefly 'chickens' (pinnated and sharp-tailed grouse). Their numbers varied noticeably in different seasons and there were sometimes quite enough to be something of a menace to our grain stooks. I don't know how it may be now but unless the present generation is more sportsmanlike than we were, there must be little enough of that quality to be seen. We were not wholly to blame. We were out to get something for the pot. Ammunition, though cheap enough positively as compared with today, was too costly for moneyless folk such as we to be lightheartedly blown away in target practice to make ourselves expert shots. It has probably always been so in communities like ours. For although practically everybody could shoot and some were really remarkable shots at long range, I only knew of one old fellow among our Canadian and American farmer friends who could take prairie chickens on the wing. He could do it well, very seldom missing.

With regard to the sportsmanship of 'raising' a bird in preference to shooting it sitting, I never even heard it claimed by anyone, whether truly or falsely, as his customary practice. Our old neighbour aforementioned would take a sitting shot if he got the chance. I have heard of it as a very rigid English sporting convention only violated by the sort of outsider who would shoot a fox but I never recollect seeing it done. Shooting for the pot as we did, in stray half-hours stolen (at that season) from our harvest fields, our technique was the precise reverse. We crept up on our quarry as quietly as possible and manoeuvered for a chance not to throw our shot away. We couldn't afford to. While engaged in these unchivalrous arts, I once shot at a prairie chicken which was standing on a fence. When I picked the bird up I found that one leg was gone completely. The limb must surely have been bitten off by a coyote or the like, level with the body and as cleanly as a surgeon's knife could have done it. The old scar was plainly visible. How the bird subsisted during the healing period passes understanding.

On what proved to be the very last occasion I went shooting before leaving the homestead, I was out about sunset one still evening in mid-September after some duck in a small and shallow lake-slough. I could hear them as they fed, dabbling in the weeds. I was making for a familiar spot where I anticipated being able to see them. At this precise moment an old Polish acquaintance hovered in sight: "VAT! YOU LOOK FOR DOOCKS (QUACK, QUACK, quack, quack, quack, quack!!!)." I fought an almost ungovernable urge toward justifiable homicide and turned sadly homeward.

The old fellow whom I have mentioned as a good wing shot had a hunting experience of a somewhat different character. He had been out with the gun one long spring afternoon, but fruitlessly, and was returning home empty handed. Quite unknown to him, a recently arrived American neighbour had almost immediately before put out some sheet iron decoy geese uncannily resembling the dark-necked gray Brant goose. The old man caught sight of them in the grass near the owner's house and stiffened to attention, electrified at the sight! Creeping up in the approved manner, utilizing every wisp of cover to bring him into range, he was horror stricken by the spectacle of the farm dog, which had just then detected him, breaking forth into barks and yelps that brought the dog's mistress to the window. The hunter, in sheer agonies of dread, gesticulated frantically for her to recall the wretched animal. Realizing the cause of it all she did so choking down her torrents of mirth as best she might. Scarcely daring to hope, the hunter was overjoyed to see the geese had not shifted ground. He crept within easy range and 'gave 'em both barrels'. His aim was accurate. The resounding clang and the gales of laughter from within doors as the geese received his broadside unflinchingly, brought the hideous truth home to the unhappy marksman. The old man was something of a local terror. There were few within range who had not writhed beneath the lash of his bitter tongue, from his family onward, but following this episode it was some time before his sarcasms ceased to be rather cheap in the market.

As a general thing, I fancy we were fairly conscientious in our observance of close season game regulations. Probably, if one knew everything, this arose less from a native self-restraint than from a general fear of being caught at the wicket by somebody else. Common sense is a help in these matters. There are few rural dwellers who are not aware to begin with that there is little to be gained by killing bird or beast in the rearing season. Almost the first stranger we met at our farmer host's on taking up our abode there was the local game warden and magistrate, an "English (middle-class) aristocrat." He entertained us with a recital of an encounter with a magnificent out-of-season buck that very week on the hills near his home. His account was really a very vivid little essay in literary suspense. "I raised my gun, and felt I must shoot. . . . I felt I must. . . . I knew I mustn't. . . . " Finally he turned his horse's head and rode sorrowfully away, not daring to look back.

This final conclusion was (later) pronounced by certain cynics then present at the table to be wholly fictitious. These judges included some whom we discovered later never allowed any principle to control their impulses. Their opinion was that the tale was really told as a 'feeler' to ascertain if we — five miles away — had any knowledge of the truth. I have always though this a good example of the credulity of the sceptic. The two critics were shrewd and cunning but both of them liars by rooted habit, and a liar merely sees another liar in every person he meets. The mere prudence of honesty being the best policy would plainly dictate the safe course; detection would have been irretrievably damning in a magistrate. Shots among

76

those game haunted hills and woods along the Blindman River where he lived would have been fatal in the close season and he would have had infinite difficulty in hiding his tracks. Neither was it at all likely that this was his first temptation. About that very time we ourselves on a berry picking expedition on the Blindman just below the magistrate's home were startled by a *wuf!* on the other side of a huge saskatoon bush. We had disturbed a big black bear from his feast of saskatoons which he appreciated as much as we did. During all the years I knew Gregory (the magistrate), I never heard any other suspicion cast upon his integrity.

During our first winter or two, one or two fellows went off annually in December to Buffalo Lake for a load of fish. They might better have gone to the big "Fish Lakes" farther north for whitefish unless it was that these were being fished to death. For Buffalo Lake contained nothing better than pike and a large part of the catch frequently consisted of mere 'suckers' which were even less esteemed. As I have observed above concerning moose meat, both were palatable enough to hungry men out in the cold all day. I have relished a platterful, smoking hot, under such conditions, but as our fare improved, I imagine we became more finicky or fastidious. The annual fishing trip apparently died a natural death.

Turning from sport to subsistence pure and simple, our principal meat diet in the earlier years, apart from rabbit, was pork. It took some little time before an ordinary man with a modest beginning of a cow or two could turn off a beef steer of the requisite size and age for slaughter and longer still before so important an item in capital or revenue account could be nonchalantly slain for home consumption. It generally had to be sold like an Irishman's pig, to meet other liabilities. It was not until a year or two that the pigs themselves were more freely available for they required a more intensive feeding both to grow and fatten them. This had first to be raised since no pig could be allowed to range at large without disaster to crops. All this required additional land to be broken and fenced. The summer 'hog-lot' was the heaviest single work of its kind on the place. Ordinary rails were of little good. This was made of young logs notched into one another, with a heavy 'rider' on top, to preclude disruption and escape by the inmates; a construction obviously not feasible at a moment's notice.

Sheep were then hardly safe in the scrub country without a fence proof against coyotes. This generally meant a woven one. In addition to this there must also — in our area at least — be abundance of fodder, and shelter both strong and comfortable against the weather. There was only one flock of sheep known to me in our locality, over a wide territory. This belonged to the gentleman who was a very well known auctioneer and a familiar figure at the annual pedigreed stock sales in the province. He was a relatively wealthy man with many original (and successful) ideas and he could afford to humour his fancies and pay for anything he chose to have.

As our resources increased, even though slowly and the economic pressure began to ease a little, we followed the very general practice of killing a beef animal for the winter and selling a part. I well remember the terrible winter of 1906-1907; nobody who endured it is likely to forget it! It was an endless succession of driving storms and long cold spells — not 'snaps' by any means! It was either the third or fourth Monday in January 1907 (21st or 28th), that we had the coldest night I ever remember in Alberta. The official thermometer at Lacombe registeed 68° below zero that night; one hundred degrees of frost. As we were feeding our stock that evening, not then knowing the actual temperature, I remarked that to stand still and breathe that air choked one as it would to run on an ordinary cold day of thirty or forty below. Any work outdoors was hard work that winter and we did an immense amount of bush work getting out logs for lumber at a small local mill, in addition to our hay-hauling and next summer's firewood.

During some six months from December to May, the three of us — my mother, my brother and myself — consumed a good sized pig and three quarters (one hind and two fore) of a two-year-old steer, a well grown, fat little beast. My mother of course in the nature of things did not eat quite as we did but even she more often than not had to go in our absence and feed her fowls those bitter January evenings. I can recall even now the huge dishes which loaded our table on our arrival home, ravenous, and the havoc we made of them. I was one of a gang of sixteen men on the Chipman hay camp in 1902, who cleaned up four big beef steers in eight weeks — in summer. I imagine our home performance was well up to that average. We were inured to icy winds and well fortified within. On our 'bush' days we had shelter once we reached the woods. Even that awful winter there were few days that we should have been out that we were not. We disdained the cold.

The most difficult period of the year from the housekeeper's angle, in seeking to provide something of variety in diet, was from the opening of spring up to about the middle of June. Even in a good cold roothouse the potatoes by this time were becoming decidedly oldish; in a house cellar unappetizingly so. Quite commonly they were the only vegetables remaining, and often had to be half boiled and browned in the oven to make them endurable. As now, garden salads, whenever they were sown, did not really begin to grow in earnest until about May 15th or so and cooking vegetables were seldom even showing above ground by that date. Spinach and chard, strangely enough, were then hardly heard of. That habit of spinach for the young of the citizenry was quite unknown amongst us. Nettles, which in the British Columbia woodlands are often available from the latter half of January onwards, were rather scarce except in certain favoured spots in the scrublands and I never heard of anyone cooking them as is frequently done on the Pacific Coast. It is not probable that our old-timers were at all well read in the French Revolution but the gathering of nettles for the pot is used (probably by non-participating scholars) as almost the final demonstration of the peasant poverty of the *ancien regime*. Our earliest greens were the well known garden weed, 'Lamb's quarter' or alternatively pigweed, an admirable substitute for spinach.

One of the old-timers, the lawyer-brother of the aforementioned magistrate, Gregory, in addition to eating mushrooms — as most of us did when we had the chance — experimented widely with the prairie fungi at large. His example was followed in later days by a well known theological scholar Dr. A.D. Miller of St. Stephen's College, Edmonton. Both investigators declared (each in his own day) that practically all the Alberta fungi were quite safely eatable. The acknowledged circumstance that both experimenters kept antidotes conveniently close at hand perhaps tended to damp the ardor of the uninitiated.

Homestead and outbuildings, Lacombe area

12

Trails

It appears to be very much of a fixed impression with many people, reasoning backward from the highways of today in contrast with the early trails, that when we had nothing else than trails we must have been in a lamentable condition. Nothing could be more completely misleading. From the times indeed, say for convenience about 1900, when settlement and fencing began to confine us to the impossible geometric road allowances, such an idea was broadly a correct conception of what actually happened. Previous to that time, we could generally go where we pleased which is the first essential of a good (natural) route. With a few occasional exceptions, the man who can do that will be found to have a good road.

Trailmaking is not so much an art as an instinct. The man who is born with it needs no instruction. Speaking broadly, the man who is not will seldom place himself voluntarily in a position where such a faculty is of any great importance. For he can seldom be induced to go any distance from the pathway some predecessor had broken for him. After many years both of historical investigation and of wide field observation with the camera, I entirely disbelieve in the picturesque supposition of human pathways on this continent as a whole having originally been paths of wild animals. I reject even more emphatically the idea which apparently lies behind this, that without such a forerunner man could not have found his way about his world.

The great animal representative of the process on this continent is the buffalo. The advocates of this theory want to prove too much. They claim for the buffalo that he always picked the firmest and most solid ground to support his enormous weight. They also want him to have the credit for always keeping to the most level courses, exactly as would a railway surveyor. In fact they give the buffalo such titles as 'untaught engineers of nature'.

Unfortunately, the buffalo champions want to eat their cake and have it. One or the other of those propositions may serve. When they are brought together each one nullifies the other. In large areas of the great buffalo habitat, and most particularly in the vast woodland territory east of the Mississippi River — the very region where this argument has been most persistently urged — the most level courses were not dry and the driest and firmest courses were not level. As an actual question of fact, both from historical testimony and from still existent visible evidence from the buffalo country itself (of which I have a considerable collection), the buffalo did both.

They went anywhere and everywhere at their own sweet will, and their trails can be found side by side, one leading to the best and the other leading to the very worst situation conceivable for a road. It is a part of the same wild theorizing that wherever a trail happens to cross a stream, we are told that there the ford was first 'discovered' and pointed out to the human occupants of the locality by the wild animals. This supposition overlooks two important considerations. The first is that river fords are forever changing in countless streams and this is particularly true in the great buffalo rivers of the West, as any number of the early pioneers have told us. The second is that practically all animals are swimmers. This applies to trailmakers and non-trailmakers alike and includes even the *felidae* (cats).

I have worked also with too many old pioneer woodsmen and plainsmen to give much credence to the notion of this type needing or following any such guide. These men, like preceding generations of the same class, had frequently or commonly an objective of their own which may not have been that of the wild creatures. I have seen quite sufficient of new trail broken out by men who had no visible previous path of any character to guide them and who I am quite certain had never even heard of the supposition of any pathfinding wild animal predecessor. It is possible to speak here with first-hand authority. For I have done that very thing myself and ten or fifteen years before my earliest introduction to the wild animal theory.

Such men were essentially very much as we ourselves were: brought up under broadly modern (i.e. nineteenth century) civilized conditions. We were, strictly speaking, men *in* the wilderness rather than men *of* the wilderness. Despite this, as a type we could adapt ourselves quite readily to outdoor pioneer life; there were very very few among the younger men, whatever their origin, who literally could not learn to find their own way around. When I consider these things, I shall require some really relevant evidence to convince me that the actual early pioneer man on this continent, the Indian, was dependent upon the self-same prey that he could successfully trap or trick, to show him how to move around his environment in safety! In most cases I suspect the advocates of this conception of the prehistoric hunter are really recording their own utter helplessness without some such external guidance as that which they predicate as a necessity for others.

Many of these trailmaking problems which are supposedly beyond human capacity to solve without an animal pilot or forerunner are really nothing more serious than the application of plain common sense. If one is leading a pack pony or driving a wagon team in a certain general direction across country in forest land or heavy scrub and finds his chosen route is heading him directly into some huge tree or dense thicket, it isn't necessary — if one is fit to be turned loose without a keeper to begin with — to call upon the ghost of some long dead buffalo or vanished Indian to help him out! Such a man turns aside from his course to where the jungle growth is thinner and dodges around the obstacle. Similarly, if some impossibly steep hill stares him in the face, he does precisely (without the engineer's instruments, which are only needful for exact calculations) what the railway surveyor does in a corresponding situation. He worms his way along or around it.

If trees must be cut, he can generally detect some nearby spot where trees are smaller and growth is thinner on the ground. Unless our pioneer is already buried in a primeval forest, such scantier spots reveal themselves in the outline contours of the treetops. If any freighter with twenty-four hours' experience on the trail cannot reason for himself that such a scantier spot will not only be drier and firmer by the circumstance of admitting more sun but also drier and harder *ipso facto* from being unable to grow trees as large and shady as the woods at large around it, then he should never (and probably would never) have left civilization! If such a spot existed within range of vision, those old pioneers could generally be trusted to find it.

The 'eye for country', whether in plainsman or engineer, is really common sense. The same principles apply in open country. If the general direction the pioneer is following brings him squarely on to some miry pothole, what about it? He isn't travelling at sixty miles an hour where it is dangerous to swing suddenly aside. He curves around the hole and back on to his general course once again.

In older lands such as England these common sense (and commonplace) practices have been, so to say, embalmed for our later observation in the ancient winding roads of the land. The trees through which the mediaeval wagoner wormed his way have been cut down. The swamp which turned him aside from his course is now drained and is merely a slight hollow in a well-tilled field or grassland. The village for which the modern traveller is aiming shows its old church tower in full view a mile or more straight before him. Yet the road winds this way and that to get there. In Canada we have very largely destroyed such memorials. Our trails in the earlier days were precisely of this character. The reason we can no longer see them as we drive though the West at large is because the straight road allowances have almost entirely swept them away. The old trails have long ago been ploughed over or turned into grass pasture beyond recovery in countless instances even by an old-timer. For the later investigator they are lost beyond conjecture or even suspicion.

The first vital requisite of the old trail, as with any natural unmade road, was firmness. This meant and always means dryness since water is 'Public Enemy No. I' of all roads, made or unmade. In the soft black loam of Northern Alberta, this firmness could only be secured by doing as men in undrained lands have done since time began wherever soft soils were the local terrain. They made their pathways on the higher levels. When there was no water passage to be crossed, such high level routes were just as relatively flat and easy along the crest or slope of a ridge as lower ones along its base. When either a real creek or watercourse or any lesser boggy depression presents itself, the nearer to its head such a water channel can be passed, the easier will the passage be and infinitely more so than farther down, where it is both deeper and wider. It has been pointed out that in England by keeping to the watersheds one can walk from the Lincolnshire 'Wash' to the Channel in Devon, a distance of well over two hundred miles, without crossing a bridge or wetting his shoes.

On a high level trail of this character, when one of the soft spots was encountered, the team came to it comparatively fresh. On a fairly well travelled trail they had been rolling along easily for any distance from three to ten miles. Here the driver commonly swung aside a little if the ground permitted to where the surface was not too badly cut up for his horses. He would chirrup to his team and with an astonishingly heavy load they would be through it (one can't say over it!) in no time. The trail at once made for the ridge or slope levels again. Except for top-heavy loads such as hay, a smooth side hill trail on firm ground was infinitely preferable to a transversely level one on a soft bottom. Even with hay, one or two human counterweights or 'outriggers' riding outside the hayrack on the high side enabled some very steep side hills to be successfully negotiated.

I never remember anyone having to be 'taught' these principles, any more than one needs to be taught to come in out of the wet. The man who would need to be taught would probably be incapable of learning. The man with no sense of locality might very easily take the wrong trail but you couldn't get him away from some trail!

Where the aforementioned soft spots were such as made turning aside difficult or virtually impossible, as for example in a flat, swampy, bushy or timbered creek, or in a soft wood, we had other methods. Long before definite bridges — even of local material — had made their appearance amongst us, or perhaps where a bridge was a constructional impossibility, or too expensive a project for one man's use on his own place, we laid down a 'corduroy' or, to be more definite, a causeway of corduroy. This was constructed on the general principles of the well known corduroy roads of the Eastern forest territories but may not perhaps have been so solidly built. Ours consisted of stout poles laid close together crossways and commonly held in place at each end by stakes driven downward to keep the wagon wheels from kicking the poles loose in coming on or off. The poles themselves would hold up the load, but to preclude teams from putting their feet through (with possible disastrous consequences) the poles where covered with smaller brush or straw and then sometimes with a top layer of sods or dirt. In its basic princiles, this expedient is of an inconceivable antiquity.

On a much heavier and more elaborate scale, this procedure has been largely followed on many Western railway routes in getting across marshy places. It is the famous device used by George Stephenson in crossing Chat Moss and has been used on other English main lines, notably the East Coast ('high speed') route to Scotland. Earlier than any railway, it was utilized by eighteenth century English roadmakers before Stephenson was born. As a boy in England, the writer lived on "Friars Causeway" in the old Roman city of Leicester, an ancient street centuries old built on the causeway by which the Black Friars (Dominicans) made their way across the swampy riverside lands to Northgate, the northern highway out of the town. On this Western continent its more immediate ancestors were the Santa Fe and the Oregon Trails, and those around the Red River. On all these this was the standard procedure.

The principal trail in Alberta was the Edmonton Trail running from Calgary. For seven years after the railway reached Calgary this was still the only short route to Edmonton. Like the later road allowances, this was a surveyed trail, under Dominion expropriation rights, independent of township surveys. There was this difference, however. The two places lie northeast and southwest of one another, and a direct route consequently runs incompatibly with the regular road allowance lines. The surveyors happily made no attempt to lay out a literally straight beeline. While surveying a direct route they followed the country on the principle I have described. At certain roughly recurring distances the trail and the road allowances tended to converge. Lacombe was about one of these. One of my earliest local recollections is of Post Office notices of so-and-so having applied for Departmental permission to divert a specified section of the trail so many yards on to the adjacent road allowance and to close up that portion which now ran through his place — "If no good cause were shown . . . " (etc., etc.). I am unaware whether any of these was ever successfully contested; in fact I never heard of even any attempted protest. If granted, this gave the applicant an integral farm with four more additional acres.

13

Tough Sleddin'

The year 1896 put me not simply beyond the mere aspirants to manhood status, but almost on the threshold of attainment, into what one might count as associate rank. I had assisted a neighbour on a longish cattle drive to a new stamping ground. This enterprise included swimming the bunch across a flooded stream and other little incidentals which established some increased degree of confidence, and gave me some valuable insights into bovine mentality which proved instructive in later days of buffalo researches, as yet unforeseen.

A later trip in the same year proved more momentous. I left home on Monday, November 2, to drive a yoke of oxen to Calgary, a distance of one hundred and twenty miles. The oxen were our own. They were being traded for a team of horses which my brother and myself were to bring up from Calgary on the return trip. There was no wagon going as we didn't yet possess one. For coming back we intended to build a 'jumper', a homemade cutter or light sleigh since by then we could anticipate snow. The oxen had their harness but without any bits as they were accustomed to being controlled by lines around their horns while I tramped behind them. I expected to cover twenty miles a day.

The first two days went fairly according to schedule. I made my forty miles plus a detour of six miles where a wrong turn led me into a sheer labyrinth of homesteaders' little wagon trails leading to nowhere except back to Red Deer again, to which town I had to retrace my steps before I could start again properly. I had been put up each night by generous farmers, well aware that they might find themselves in similar need some day. They also gave me guidance for the next day's journey.

Shortly after noon the third day, it began to snow. Although I was not then aware of it, this was actually the beginning of the winter's snow, and we never saw the ground again for over five months. I was yet some eight miles from Jack Urquhart's, a regular stopping house where I was advised to camp for the night, as the next house was eleven miles farther on and not given to housing stoppers. I fortunately had the storm at my back but by the time I reached Urquhart's the snow was well up toward knee deep, and blowing and drifting hard. I tied up there gladly and put my oxen in their barn. Next morning the snow was anything from knee deep to thigh deep and still coming! I had seventeen miles ahead of me and another thirteen between there (Chamberlain's) and the next stopping-house (Freeze's). There was no provender for my oxen until we reached one of these, although they could eat snow for a drink. The trail was just visible ahead of me, an unbroken streak of whiter-than-white. We started at daylight. My oxen had had a comfortable night and were well fed and in good heart. They were renowned for good pacers and they stepped out well. I didn't stop anywhere for eating since there was none for my team, but pushed along and munched a bite out of my little sack, half frozen.

When I came to Chamberlain's there were still two hours of daylight left. I hated to lose this since I'd heard of a sheep ranch not so far out of my road where I might perhaps stick up for the night. Just as dusk was settling in, a well worn hay trail cut into my route and gave my oxen a little respite from trail breaking, which had been their lot since dawn. Night fell and I was dubious where this hay trail might mislead me. There was an enormous haystack just discernible a little off the main trail I had been following. Fortunately when I got there it had been opened and there was loose hay in abundance. I put my oxen on the leeward side, wound their lines firmly about my middle, and burrowed myself in deeply. Once in the night they scared about something, perhaps a coyote, but I got them quietened again and they stayed put till morning. When I turned out it was crystal clear, the air was crackling, and umpteen below zero. I shook for the first mile or two until my feet warmed up a little. I met one man who in answer to my inquiries said that Freeze's was "just about five miles" which is the stock distance from anywhere on the plains. I hiked between seven and eight miles (as I long afterwards verified) and all at once over a low shoulder of hill there was Freeze's below me! I marched up to the door and asked the motherly looking dame if I might give my oxen a feed. This good lady knew her mileages. She looked hard at me, and then said, "Where did you put up last night? I know you haven't come from Chamberlain's, you haven't had time." I told her I'd slept in the haystack. "You go straight and put those oxen in the barn and see they get a good feed and come right back to the house." When I reached the house the very biggest beef steak I think I've ever seen was sizzling in the pan, something like fifteen inches square and over an inch thick, with fried potatoes and other trimmings in attendance. She was all alone; the men were out. Stoppers were a part of their living but she wouldn't take a cent. She not only filled me within serious danger of collapse, she also gave me fresh stores of hot beef sandwich for my (frozen) grubsack. And finally she gave me careful directions to call without fail at the first house I should strike on the east side of the trail. This was an old Englishman and his wife from Salisbury who never turned anybody away. When I got there I should be only five miles from Calgary. I have never forgotten her abounding goodness and I never shall.

All went according to Hoyle. I found her friend, who fed my oxen and myself sumptuously. The old gentleman was a dyed-in-the-wool Anglican but all the same his closest friend out in the West was "Fred Locke," a devoted Methodist minister with a roving circuit across the cow country (which couldn't support stationary ministers on that scanty population). Fred Locke's 'parish' was some sixty by sixty miles across, a man who was hail-fellow-well-met everywhere. I had the pleasure of meeting Fred Locke's son nearly half a century later, Dr. F.W. Locke of Lacombe, right in my own country.

I had not been in Calgary since our first arrival in the country. It was beginning to think itself sufficiently sophisticated to stare at the spectacle of a travel worn hick plodding up Main Street with a yoke of oxen. It proved sufficiently modern that my ultimate destination, a few miles out, supposed to be known to everyone, rang no bell in anybody I encountered. It took me all day to get out eight miles. I finally made it however to discover that as a 'kid brother' I was near famous. I'd started out with fifty cents and had twenty remaining at my journey's end!

We were held in the South longer than we had expected. It was December first before we got away. We had our jumper tolerably well laden with various commodities and stores, not forgetting a bale of hay and a sack of oats in the event of not making some stopping house for the night. We had only one horse instead of the expected team. His mate had strayed off to the range or had possibly (as we suspected) been sold again by her crooked owner begrudging the deal. He had undertaken to replace her with another if she was not 'recovered'.

The weather had turned warmer as it often did in December and we anticipated a decent trip. The day before we started, however, there blew up a chinook, a violent one, such as are much more common to the South country than to our own home region. The local traffic into town had beaten it into a splendid sleigh road. For some five miles we made good trotting time and were in high spirits. At the very last of the local settlers' houses our good trail suddenly petered out and ahead of us was a pathless waste such as I had struggled through coming southward. We had to take turns breaking a way for our horse, well nigh thigh deep in the snow. Instead of making Freeze's (the Lady of the Beef steak), when it finally became too dark to see our way we were only at the Buttes', eight miles short of our desired haven. At this point the snow had blown clear from a small rocky shoulder and we knew we were on the trail. But right close below us were the headwaters of Nose Creek with springs and potholes fifteen feet deep even in summertime without any snowdrifts. If we slid into those, neither horse nor man would have a dog's chance. We daren't take any chances; we decided to camp where we were.

I don't think I ever passed a more miserable night in my life. The temperature wasn't low, little more than freezing, but there was a damp, raw, ragged wind that went through one and came out on the other side. We had no fire, for there was nothing in the vicinity bigger than a matchstick. We tramped back and forward over that tiny windswept spot from 4:30 p.m. till 8:00 a.m. Tramp till you reeled from weariness; squat down and doze until you woke up shaking! Watching the Great Bear circling two-thirds of the vast circle, and crawling as though to let the snails whizz by! Our good friend in the shafts was the best served of the company. He was snugly blanketed, munching-and-sleeping and sleeping-and-munching in high contentment through the dismal night. With the very earliest gleam of light we were up and away. It took five hours to make the eight miles to Freeze's.

Two p.m. — it was too soon to tie up for the night; seventeen miles over such a trail to Chamberlain's was too far so we decided to try for the sheep ranch; "he sometimes takes pilgrims in" was Mrs. Freeze's unencouraging verdict. The genial head himself, a Caledonian as dour as he looked (which is saying something) was fully prepared to deny us and began reciting various (low) mileages to somewhere else, but my brother had revived an old neuralgia as a result of our night-and-day vicissitudes, and the ranch house gang staged a sort of mild mini-mutiny and took the law into their own capable hands. So we spent a quasi-comfortable night in an atmosphere like a baker's oven operating in a Turkish bath. We turned out into a bright morning colder than ever.

The ranch house stood in just about the same 'latitude' as my nocturnal haystack, so from there to Urquhart's was the exact reverse of my day's work on the southbound trip. We made Urquhart's at dark, and this time I (who acted as Introducer, by right of prior knowledge) was in a somewhat better position to speak with the enemy in the gate. Old Jack had only hit me for thirty cents on the way down — for my oxen — I went free. Once again we bedded down comfortably and the neuralgia calmed down a little. The next morning we had a solid spell of some ten miles or so without any vestige of a broken trail. Urquhart told me that nobody had gone by since the storm broke. The 'drummers' working the territory had evidently preferred to trust to the railroad, certainly until somebody else broke the trail for them, and there was then no organized snow plough service for highways in the country. What we actually had to face this day was the toughest of all our snow bucking. In the course of this day's trek we had to cross the aforementioned frontier between the baldheaded prairie and the scrub lands. Very much as the great cliffs of Western Ireland and the Biscay seaboard confront the giant Atlantic seas with their first positive stop, so here the sweeping blizzards of the plains met their first fixed obstacle. And here there was a wide tract of snow flanking the woods, varying in depth from thigh deep to belly deep on the level and, thanks to the recent Chinook, just soft enough that it wouldn't hold us up, and sticky enough that it couldn't be kicked aside.

We were in a lonely land. For some thirty-five miles the Edmonton Trail and the railway — nominally parallel — were three or four miles apart. There was no help to be looked for from settlers driving in from their homes to the local towns. We had to break trail ahead of our horse over a stretch of some ten miles which included some fearful plunging, from daylight till dark, and this with a sick man suffering agonies in the jumper. Then a strange thing happened.

When we struck the northern scrub and timber area, which we did just before total darkness came on, a little south of the 'Lone Pine', an old abandoned pre-railway stage station, we were in settled territory once more and the thick timber had defied the fury of the storm. All at once we found a broad and well travelled sleigh road under our feet. We were at this time about ten miles from the town of Innisfail. Our horse was young, well fed and in first class hardened condition. Despite all this one might well wonder if that day's terrific toils hadn't worn him out. So far from that, he no sooner felt the good clear road under his feet than he broke into a spanking trot and whirled us into Innisfail in no more than an hour, as though he had just been brought forth from the stable and I had my first ride since leaving the travelled trails north of Calgary. We had been five long days making sixty-five miles: in 1955 I travelled the same stretch by "Dayliner" in seventy minutes with one or two intermediate stops.

On the well established principle of flogging the willing horse, we again sought shelter with my hosts of the southbound trip and were not refused. We turned out next morning into a frozen world of two colours only. Everything above us was an almost aching blue and everything around us was an aching white, glittering with thick hoar frost, and cold. We were still forty miles from home but the roads were good and man and beast were in good fettle. We made Red Deer, the first twenty, easily by noon. The cloudless blue had become overcast with a nasty wind in our faces. Mid-afternoon or thereabouts we were to pass a friend's place. We decided rather foolishly to stop off and warm up with possibly an overnight invitation in the offing to avoid waking my mother after she had probably turned in. But instead of due supplication at the outset, my brother — more particularly the friend of our host — waited for the latter to invite us and he didn't! At last, when it must have been perfectly clear what we were waiting for, he explained to us somewhat laboriously and quite unconvincingly (for a shake-down on the floor would have been admirable) that he was short of a second bed. So we had to turn out again into the cold and cruel night!

But we were in a different country now. Four or five miles ahead of us was the Blindman River bush, with an infinitude of firewood. Camping there for the night was no hardship so with our friend comfortably blanketed and a huge fire we spent the midnight hours luxuriously. On the last leg of our trip and only five miles from home we were breakfasted gorgeously by a friend who would take no denial. We reached home just before noon to my mother's great joy since she'd heard nothing from me during the weeks, postal communications having been somewhat erratic during the stormy interlude. I rather think this midwinter trip greatly impressed some of our Canadian friends who had seemed to wonder if we'd got what it takes.

There is one final incident that deserves telling. Before leaving home I had cut for my mother a goodly pile of firewood such as by any conceivable standards would be more than ample for the fortnight or so that I expected to be absent. The month of November, however, had been a succession of bitter sweeping storms with nights of deadly cold. Our log house on my mother's place (which the Department had allowed her to take over conditionally upon completing the homestead duties), the lineal successor of the original sod shack, stood out in the unsheltered open like its predecessor. The storms of that awful month, which in themselves made the fires burn more wastefully, kept her shovelling in wood (only cookstove size), which diminished the pile at an alarming rate. Sometimes the fire had to be additionally fed during the night. Eventually a very stormy Sunday brought her to her very last fire. She put it into the stove and then knelt down to pray. She had barely risen from her knees when there came a knock at the door. She opened it and there stood a brawny young fellow, the son of her nearest neighbour, half a mile away. "We were just sitting down to dinner when it suddenly struck me — 'I wonder just

how old Mrs. Rowe is fixed for firewood.' So here I am."
There was plenty by the house and I needn't add that she had
no further anxiety on that score. I have told the foregoing
exactly as she told it to me.

Several years later my mother had the opportunity to
repay the debt in rather dramatic fashion. The same young
fellow and his wife were wrestling with their first born's initial
siege of tummy ache. During some hours of affliction their
home had been anything but a Temple of Peace with the
unversed young mother vainly endeavouring to soothe her
suffering child. My mother said, "Give him to me for a
moment." She turned the baby over onto his aching tummy
and in about three minutes he was sound asleep! I think their
gratitude eclipsed the utmost she could possibly have felt, even
for the woodcutting. Both father and son died within the last
four or five years.

14

Snow

At first sight the idea of writing historically about snow in Alberta seems merely grotesque. For during half the year snow in Alberta, potentially at least, is like the poor — always with us. Yet somehow one feels that psychologically the Alberta angle of approach to snow has changed, together with the material and visible change from the horse to the internal combustion engine, from the bobsleigh to the truck. At best, snow is a mere nuisance, an impediment in the path of the wheels. To obviate this, the highways— actually *high ways* wherever practicable, like their essential trail prototypes for ages back, have been built up to preclude drifting wherever this can be effected. Where it cannot, the highway requires extra protection, all of which signifies heavier taxation for its maintenance. At the worst — if snow brings cold weather which renders highway driving more difficult and dangerous, it becomes a positive and active enemy. It is very seldom a friend to the modern man.

To us the snow was decidedly a friend and perhaps more so than we were at times ungratefully inclined to acknowledge, particularly in the wet years when freeze-up came and we could at last journey over the bogs instead of having to struggle through them. Even before the wet cycle, when a well travelled trail over firm ground made a most excellent road for horse vehicles (as it now does for motors), there were other trails which were not sufficiently main routes for the traffic to smooth them down very materially. In the bush sections some of these were very rough with roots and stumps. For a stump which had originally been cut level with the ground ceased to be so after wheels had packed and ground their surrounding soil down a few inches. If this was their condition in summer,

96

winter's frost made them even harder and bumpier. I remember on one occasion my mother holding a precious pane of glass on her knee for ten miles. She had gone with me for this particular purpose and since we could not obtain (nor even borrow) a crate, she wrapped the glass in a thick rug and held it. On a stretch of bush trail, after dark and within a mile of home, the wheel found a root. The glass was literally broken over her knee into fragments.

A co-operative effort sometimes bridged or corduroyed some particularly bad spot which a lot of us must use. Our two days of road work (tax, paid in labour) only served as it was for the very worst places. It was ten years before our efforts ceased to be exclusively volunteer. Furthermore, even in the earlier days before we were driven entirely to the road allowances, we were often compelled or even induced to change our trails. Some later purchaser would fence up a hitherto beeline trail across lots. Nearer home, perhaps, a similar purchaser in the centre of a wide unsettled tract had to break out his own trail to the nearest 'main line' which was thereby made nearer than the one we had thus far been using. A mile or less of this intervening trail would put several of us on this superior route. for such reasons we were loath to put too much effort into long stretches of local trails until we could feel sure it was not being wasted.

Snow settled all these problems for us overnight. It is true of course that immediately around our own doors, where we had our own familiar beaten paths, a deep snowfall made the going heavier for a few days until we got it beaten down again. There were also times when we would have liked to finish some job, and of course if we had a 'brushing' campaign in prospect, deep snow put the veto on that. But its benefits in the days of the log-and-rail economy far outweighed its disadvantages and particularly to those who, like myself, were commonly working single-handed. An enormous proportion of our winter work consisted of heavy lifting and heavy hauling to somewhere else. With considerable labour, a man could go to the woods and bring home a load of rails on a wagon, if he could get in and out again. But only with sleighs could a single-handed man bring home a piled up load of heavy logs.

Not all of us had a wagon apiece in the old days and plenty of men had wagons — analogous to a T-model Ford —

that none but an incurable optimist would dare to take to the woods. But anyone who had anything to pull it with could have a sleigh! Even if he was so poor that he couldn't afford having it shod with band iron, the runners could be made rather thicker and left 'in the round'. A glance around town in the earlier winters revealed that factory made 'bobs' were in the minority. We ourselves were eight years before we had them. We knew of many things on which we could well have spent the money but we got the bobs first and afforded them after. For we were utterly fed up with homemade softwood substitutes fashioned from the local materials.

It will readily be seen that plenty of snow meant much with a homemade sleigh of that description. Whatever made the drawing harder increased the strain on the sleigh just as much as on the team. Plenty of snow in the bush also meant a better chance among the dead fallen trees which lay underfoot in all directions and which would snap a softwood runner like a matchstick if one crossed it with a load. In those days, while walking or driving through the woods, we were constantly on the alert for crooked trees suitable for curved sleigh runners. Happy were we if the sooner-or-later inevitable smash found us with a spare 'crook' in stock! Otherwise everything was held up while we hunted here, there and everywhere to find one. To saw a bend out of straight grain was a mere waste of effort.

We laughed over it later but it was scarcely any joke at the time. One laid out an ambitious week's work hauling out rails; two loads in the morning, two in the afternoon. The prophetic eye could see the twenty-four loads already strung out on the line. Monday — four loads, everything O.K. Second load on Tuesday morning, a broken runner. Tuesday afternoon and Wednesday, finding a suitable crook. Thursday, making a new runner. Friday, hauling in hay. Saturday, trip to town. Total for the week — five loads of rails! Time was the only thing that some of us possessed in equal shares with everybody else. In our attempts to make time serve in place of money, the rates of exchange were sometimes cruelly high. I well remember the carefree abandon with which I went to the woods after we got the factory made steel and hardwood bobsleighs, none daring to make me afraid!

One could have too much of a good thing, none the less.

To the children of today, even in many rural regions, one might almost say that snow hardly appears in their lives except as a source of pleasure. The school bus has eliminated its hardships. It was different in most of the country parts at the turn of the century. I particularly recall a passenger run on which we left Whitecourt on the Athabaska River at 7 a.m. We ran into Mayerthorpe just about as the local country children were trooping into the village school. They had manifestly come so far that they had their lunches with them. We commonly met a party at a certain crossing, tiny creatures wrapped up to the eyes, but very seldom absent! Some of those January mornings were bitter, with the cloudless air almost crackling and temperatures far below zero, or a cruel driving wind that made a mockery of higher readings as it smote upon their faces and made their steps a toil. But short of an absolute blizzard there they were! One likes to think their parents themselves prized their schooling highly enough to be willing to fight for it.

We were not the only ones that winter of 1896-97 to discover that one can have too much of such a good thing as snow. A tie-cutting enterprise blossomed on the farther side of Gull Lake. I never learned whether the promoter-in-chief had a contract or whether this was one of those optimistic visions where "the C.P.R. 'll only be too darn glad to get 'em!" The contractor-optimist had injected something of his own enthusiasms into his neighbours. For once the local woods held the key to wealth! I forget the price per tie, but "you could haul forty or fifty to a load, . . . good ice road. . ." and so forth. The hewn ties were to be hauled double-length for convenience and sawn through at Lacombe. Some hapless man started across the lake with his tonnage, twelve miles across and twelve more to Lacombe. He was caught in a storm and had to jettison his cargo progressively. He finally got across with two ties (one log), which he kept on the sleigh to sit on! *Sic transit.* . . .

It was during this same winter of 1896-97 that I first noted a phenomenon which puzzled me greatly at the time. Our southwest winds under normal conditions were invariably warm ones. That winter the occasional southwest winds were as bitter as those from the southeast, which is the acid test. Since then I have noticed the same condition in other winters

99

of excessively heavy snowfall and only then. I believe the explanation is that in blowing across hundreds of miles blanketed with snow to an abnormally heavy degree, instead of the Chinook melting the snow, the snow 'froze' the Chinook. It was notorious with us that the southeast winds which blew across open plains were much more bitterly cold than any wind we ever got from the northwest or northeast which — then at least — blew over sheltered woods.

This was our earliest winter in Alberta of that long enduring intense cold which was almost the normal winter weather in Manitoba and Saskatchewan. The winter following, 1897-98, was the same. In both years the snow fell on unfrozen ground in the first week of November and remained unbrokenly until spring. 1904-1905 and 1905-1906 were the precise reverse; two virtually snowless winters consecutively — again with no parallel known to me. In March 1897, I had my first experience of snow blindness, having to drive across an enormous expanse of unbroken white. It was not severe but quite severe enough. In March 1899, I had a much worse attack, just bad enough that I had to make a projected trip across the open prairie by night instead of day.

These winter experiences led me to conclusions which I have since seen no reason to change. The endurance of really excessively low temperatures, so that it is quite safe and natural to go forth alone, is an art which has to be learned by practice. It is in my opinion entirely independent of how well one may be fed or clad. Two men equally well equipped inside and out, will react differently. The newcomer endures it with hardness, if he endures it at all. The old-timer takes it in his stride. I was out alone on one occasion when I believe that nothing but this art of endurance got me back safely. I had to go to town one January day with a team and bob sleighs. I asked a friend whose house I passed to go with me: "No! Too cold. I'll lend you my fur coat, though." I took it and was quite comfortable. In town the official government thermometer registered at sixty-two below zero. I reached my friend's at sunset; a cloudless January evening, with the air almost crackling, and — I was so foolish as to leave the fur coat! I had a mile and a half to go in the mackinaw coat which I had worn all day beneath the fur one. In spite of running behind the team and every other trick I knew, I began to wonder if I could stick it out. I have ridden for the doctor at forty below in the small hours of January nights, but I never suffered as on that short journey. I suspect a newcomer might have gone under.

Despite those one or two early winters of abnormal snowfall, it was not until the terrific winter of 1906-1907 that I first saw a snow plough in use. This was a homemade affair of logs and plank weighted with stones. We managed with our trails getting higher and higher until April, but even then the snow hung on and the old winter trails — by then like snow walls — became at last impossible. That spring snow remained on the northern sides of the bluffs until after the beginning of May. Hence the snow plough. In 1907 my first spring ploughing (and on a hilltop!) was not until May 3rd, the latest of any year I can remember. In 1897 and again in 1898 spring thaw came about April 10-14th; otherwise we might have needed snow ploughs long before 1907.

15

A Day in Court

The prairie fires of May 1898 were almost epoch in the Red Deer canyon country. They jumped the Red Deer River while slighter barriers were almost contemptuously ignored. In a scrub-and-timber locality the thick pall of smoke blotted out local details from identification and rendered it difficult to detect their nearer or farther proximity or direction. Due to such confusions, some men found themselves fighting dangers that were not immediate, while other more vital fires might steal upon them from the flank or rear.

My mother and I were at this time residing alone on the homestead ten miles east of Blackfalds and neither of us had any experience with prairie fires and their insidious ways. But I was soon to learn. On Saturday, May 14th, I went down to my mother's homestead to plough a small field. The fence had been smashed by a bunch of range horses the previous season and the growth lay scattered in all directions; it was a mat that no plough could force its way through. Clearly the simplest thing to do was to burn this obstruction away!

It was a hot still morning when I applied the match. At that time I was simply unaware that a fire creates its own wind. Even some magistrates knew no better, since such a plea was often received as a mere lie. On this occasion it seemed in one minute as though one could cover the fire with his hand and in the next a ten-acre field wouldn't have contained it. In almost no time the fire was romping up the valley like an express train. I don't think I ever heard where it burned itself out or was stopped.

The next day, Sunday the 15th, was even more ominous. My original fire up the valley had secured us from danger on the open side but there was nothing to protect us from the forest direction. We had not yet been on the place six months and the willow scrub was tall and thick enough that it had to be cleared before a firebreak could be ploughed around the house. And it was entirely without protection if by any chance we were absent.

On the Sunday the billowing volumes of smoke looked so threatening that we felt that some effort must be made immediatcly. The house stood at the *debouchment* or outfall of a small narrow pass, a mere winding notch through the ridge. The little valley floor bore a heavy growth of grasses which would be difficult to handle if the fire came upon us. The only break was a small narrow foot trail twelve inches wide, very possibly an old buffalo trail. As I set out, my mother begged to accompany me and I agreed, more to keep her from worrying than from any real expectation that she could do very much of a positive character. Actually, however, her assistance proved invaluable.

My plan was to use the narrow path as a firebreak and to backfire southwards in the direction of the smoke. The little path itself was so overgrown with trampled grasses, however, that it had to be raked clear before I dared to light a match. My mother went before me with the garden rake and pulled the grasses over on the the southward side to be burned with my backfire. I followed with a wet sack to knock out any fragments of fire that could possibly jump my trail once the main blaze was on its way to meet the destroyer to the south. Since there was no water obtainable until we got a mile or more through the pass, I carried a pail with me to re-dampen our wet sack from time to time.

After a hurried dinner we started out about one p.m. taking nothing with us as we expected to be back in two or three hours. But it was near one a.m. when we returned, famished, weary, dirty, our eyes streaming from the smoke of our own fires, but safe, or so we fondly believed.

Alas! When I reached home I saw that the whole landscape was a blackened smoking mass. The same fire, or another, had jumped our barrier farther down or had otehwise taken us in the flank, and had roared *uphill* through the bare sun-drenched side of the pass, which became an inferno of flame that swept everything in its path and caught the matted forest growth at the summit of the climb. A fire rushing up a hill, with fresh fuel constantly *above* the flame, attains almost express speed and is the deadliest of all.

The only building that remained intact was our home. Our first little stable, put up in a hurry just a week before Christmas, was not itself consumed, but the manure banked up around the walls for warmth had burned out the corners and left a dishevelled woodpile. Two thousand rails cut and spread out in the winter along their projected fence line were reduced to mere short ends fit only for the cookstove. But our very poverty spared us one pang. Prior to attaining the dignity of an implement shed, it was a common practice to park one's implements in a small bluff where cattle would neither smash them nor get caught or gored by them. At this time, we had nothing but a wagon and a breaking plough and hence were spared greater evils.

The official sequel gave me an unwelcome sight into the formal working of law and order for I became implicated in the legalities of the fire situation. In the official terminology, I had "allowed the fire to get beyond my control" even though informed local opinion held that my fire had actually been benefit, since it facilitated the back-firing operations which ultimately extinguished the main blaze. The law, however, knew nothing of such refinements. Since my name had been "handed in," I suppose the local constabulary had no alternative.

Thursday afternoon, May 19th, Sergeant Evans of the North-West Mounted Police came riding into the farmyard. I remember his telling us Mr. Gladstone had died that day — no doubt at that time an event to thoughtful Welshman. The news had come over the C.P.R. telegraph to the *Edmonton Bulletin,* and the operator at Red Deer had 'milked' the wire. We could have waited a month for the news from English friends in the ordinary manner.

Apart from occasional exceptions (commonly ex-British sergeant-majors or the like) the off-duty police at smaller towns were men among men. Sergeant Evans, a veteran of the 1885 days, was one of the genial type. Doubtless this easy camaraderie carried its complementary sorrows. In such an uninhibited atmosphere the sergeant's appearance neither surprised nor shocked us. We knew quite well what he had come for. So did he. He made no mention of himself, but he wanted a chance of a rest and a nibble for his mare for he had ridden thirty or forty miles over a blackened wilderness that morning. Like a righteous man regardeth the life of his beast (and not knowing how far the starvation plains might extend) he carried a small sack of oats at the saddle-bow for his mount; she munched contentedly there while we entertained her rider within. He made no reference to his official errand until he had finished his own bite. Then when ready to depart, he read out to me the formal summons. He desired me to be at the magistrate's, eight miles distant, at four p.m., as he still had another call to make. The only suggestion of official menace was in his final injunction — "Fail not."

The magistrate's 'court' deserves a pen-picture beyond my feeble powers. Professor John Macoun, stated in 1882 that the Englishman preferred a picturesque location for his dwelling place, regardless of its practical deficiencies as a farm. As a complete generalization this is incorrect. It is true enough, however, of the 'remittance man'; and to this type (though not to the class) our magistrate belonged. The shack, which he shared with his lawyer-brother, stood in a terrain of miniature Dartmoors or Peaks of Derbyshire. The only level spot in the vicinity was the house floor itself. Possibly for this reason the firewood was cut up inside the house. Underfoot was a thickish carpet of chips and bark much like the floor of a coniferous forest.

The only serious architectural blemish in the interior design was that the end-gate of the cookstove should have been at the furthest extremity of the single room, directly opposite the outer door. Then the long dry trees would need only to have been cut short enough to allow the house door to close, and thence forward could have been fed into the stove a length at a time. Instead, doubtless through a deplorable lack of experience, the stove had been placed at an impossible diagonal and the firewood had to be subdivided into something like ordinary stove lengths of three to a cord. Even here, however, a considerable amount of labour saving was achieved by conducting these operations indoors and consequently there was a convenient and plentiful supply of dry kindling immediately available.

The furniture was definitely home-wrought and represented the least common denominator in that field of domestic art. If a work of art is something which fulfils the purpose for which it was designed then the table and two or three chairs might claim this status. These were constructed on strictly rectangular-parallelogramatic principles and looked not unlike sawn out cross sections of pews still to be seen in some old churches. They at least had flat arms to sit on, which furnished their only quasi-comfortable portions. The magistrate's chair was of a pattern that I think was described as Cape Cod. It had once been a flour or sugar barrel. A semi-circle had been cut away from the front at the requisite height and this portion, secured to stout cleats, made the seat with arm rests on either side. The top head of the barrel ripped across, made two rockers. A cushion on the seat met the aesthetic or osteological demands of the occupant.

The log walls were garnished with the household goods in infinite variety. A cupboard *sans* door had been promoted from its former lowlier status as a packing case and a similarly rough bookcase that a joiner would have said had been "spit together," hung precariously on the wall. The latter held the usual collection of old favourites together with paper-backed copies of later vintages, some of them indicative of unquestionable critical tastes in literature. Cheek-by-jowl with these was an assortment of chaps, saddles, bridles, bits, guns, paddles, fishing rods and winter riding gear. The artistic appeal was gratified by pin-ups of that era and cartoons from illustrated Christmas numbers of *Punch* and *The Illustrated London News*.

The table and stove were less artistically furnished, testifying to the harder practical needs of life. The teapot bore a rich dark mahogany tint outside and the hues of Erebus within. The frying pan might have passed for a model of an extinct volcano buried under snow, the congealed remaining vestiges of dynasties of steaks and rashers that had met their end there. The table was a mere uncharted wilderness of unwashed plates in obverse or reverse, knives, forks, spoons, salt and pepper, the sugar, the bottle of Lea and Perrins in active service, pipes and the book-of-the-moment flung face down at the instant of interruption.

And the magistrate? He had been sent out, I should judge in his mid-twenties, as an advanced and hopeless T.B. case, to see if the fresh air regimen might help a bit. It did. He had only one lung but to judge from appearances he might have had four! He was never seen at any time with a hat or a shirt button fastened, even when riding twenty miles an hour. His hair was not worn long in the sense of the contemporary Buffalo Bill; it was merely conventional short hair left untended. Also, I never remember seeing him except behind a barrage of auburn stubble. This, with a dragon's moustache, should certainly have rendered him an object of terror to evil-doers.

He had anticipated the modern tendency to discard the judicial wig and robe and he certainly had the courage of his convictions. His garb on this occasion was a one-piece combination undershirt, very much open at the neck and farther down. Shakespeare seems to supply the only absolutely appropriate commentary. He was to the life "the justice in fair round [and visible] belly, with eyes severe and beard of formal [though not recent] cut. ..." A prudent pair of slippers on that floor completed the picture.

I speedily discovered that I was not alone in my delinquency for another culprit was there before me. He was an American settler, a Mr. Sherwin, whom I knew very well, living some six miles to the south towards the Red Deer River. This offender had dressed up in his best, a Westernized edition of the conventional Sunday-go-to-meeting attire; in externals at least he looked much more like a magistrate than the actual officiating functionary.

My fellow victim and I had been arraigned upon the same charge. His case was taken first and it soon appeared that he was a man more sinned against than sinning. This fire of which he was most unjustly accused had in truth come upon him like a thief in the night. It was only by the most strenuous and unremitting efforts that he had been able to save his home, his wife, his children, his man servant and maid servant, his ox and his ass, and all the various goods and chattels that were his. Unfortunately, Mr. Sherwin had been seen tearing down the trail hell-for-leather into an unclouded morning totally devoid of smoke and shortly afterwards galloping back over the hill in similar haste, to be followed only too soon by a raging demon of flame that threatened more possessions than his alone. With this starting point, Sergeant Evans had unearthed somebody who had actually seen Sherwin on a recognized horse, dismount and start the fire. This was something much more than mere circumstantial evidence. Men's horses were known in those days; likewise their styles of riding. This identification closed the case.

I have mentioned the magistrate's somewhat unconventional garb. But with it all he was still The Law. When he came to deliver judgment all the extraneous unessentials fell away like water off a duck's back! I can still hear those clear cultured accents, the South of England-cum-Modified Oxford tones with all their final g's carefully enunciated. "You have been convicted upon this charge. I shall fine you twenty-five dollars and costs; and let me warn you most earnestly that if you are brought before me again on any similar charge I shall not be so lenient the next time. . . " My own case was remanded for a week.

Our homeward paths lay together for several miles along the Buffalo Lake Trail. Mr. Sherwin had done his best and failed and I've always thought he took his medicine like a man. He had come prepared for a possible conviction but he never dropped the least hint as to whether this was merely a precaution, or a real recognition that actually he hadn't a leg to stand on. He brought out his money and paid up on the spot. I did notice, however, that on our homeward ride there was never a word about "your damned British justice" or the like. All that Sherwin said to me on the subject of the day was, "Next time you go up agin' that man, you wanta make a god . . . damned . . . helluva . . . poor . . . mouth." I wonder if he ever regretted not having practised more consistently what he preached; the ultra-respectable appearance might have led to a false conception of his ability to pay. It is also perhaps not wholly impossible that Mr. Sherwin paid something for his own sartorial eclipse of the magistrate.

I came up for judgement a week later. In consideration of my age (nineteen) and being fatherless, a first offence, our recognized poverty, and having suffered myself severely from the spring fires which had destroyed everything but my home, I was bound over to keep the peace for six months. The fact that my fire had actually assisted to render control of the larger one somewhat easier, while no legal exoneration, was allowed weight. I learned later that a friend, S.W. Paisley, who was not even a close neighbour, had interceded very strongly on my behalf.

I have always suspected that both the police and the court were inclined to leniency from the beginning but felt that the outright acquittal of a born British subject and the punishment of an alien offender at the same session for an identical offence (apart from the "perjury") would leave a bad taste in the mouth. What would have happened in the event of a sentence is anybody's guess for I hadn't a cent.

16

Indians

I have sometimes been asked what the Indians were like at the turn of the century. In the essentials the aboriginal Indian of the Plains territory vanished when his age-long mainstay, the buffalo, disappeared. For it was only by means of the buffalo that he could continue to live the life of his fathers. The body of the Indian survived for a space, in the normal span of life, but the soul had fled. We occasionally saw surviving features of the old days such as the tepee and travois. I do not of course refer to these when brought out on holiday occasions as stage properties, part of the show, but of everyday life. In less picturesque relationships we naturally saw something more of them in the very earliest years than is common now. When a beef animal was killed they would take the head and offals in return for tanning the hide. This process, if performed by an expert — for they varied — would give one a robe that could be pinched like paper between finger and thumb. Moccasins could also be bought from them and these were far superior to the factory article. For in the latter the design—which is copied in the 'brogan' shoe of today—had the seams in a state of tension on the upper surface, and there is a visible strain on the thread stitches in admitting (of forcing in) a heavily stockinged foot. Whereas the Stoney or Cree moccasin was formed of one piece of deer or moose hide, doubled over portfolio fashion like the covers of a book, and stitched along the outer edges on a widish parallel with the outline of the human foot. There was no strain on the stitching since the natural pressure of the tread (with its tendency to flatten out the moccasin at each step) reduced this progressively in direct proportion to the weight of the wearer.

The heavier the Indian, the less was the strain on the seams of the moccasins. The best ones, moreover, were stitched with sinew and commonly the seams outlasted the moccasins.

I forget what were the prices when ordered 'formally' from the Indians, but they were somewhere about seventy-five cents a pair. Moccasins should really be worn as the Indians wore them; put on and never taken off again. They were not greatly favoured in the Chinook area as they became damp or wet in the 'soft spells' in winter and had to be dried (for white people), usually with serious or fatal results to the moccasins. As white men's footgear to be taken off every night as white men do, they might pass in those areas where the snows never melt or soften until the close of winter, but where rubber overshoes had either to be worn intermittently, or the unpleasant consequences of going without them had to be faced, I thought them decidedly unsatisfactory. Without doubt they have their merits on snowshoes but some such soft and yielding surface as that is almost imperative for white men's feet. To wear them at work in any woods but green conifera with their cushion of cones and needles would need a grilling apprenticeship as I can testify from experience. They were at one time rather in vogue among the remittance men as winter footgear, possibly from their romantic appeal, but the romance of an obviously or even glaringly factory made imitation soon became dimmed and the devotees of the fad became noticeably fewer. Few or many, the periodical change twice a year between moccasins and heeled shoes was pretty severe on strained or flexed leg muscles; the game wasn't worth the candle.

The only moccasins I ever bought directly from the Indians cost me fifty cents for two pairs. Had I possessed the flour, I could have got them for a cupful of the substance, which was the price I saw paid for a full-grown marten skin. These Stoneys had been away from Reservation rations all summer and had run out of flour, which they valued in the wilds more than money. This at times is perhaps not sufficiently considered in commenting on ridiculous prices paid to Indians for 'valuable' furs. But we must also remember that the Indian wasn't allowed to tell the trader what he would take for his furs. The trader said what he would give.

One thing the Indians were always ready to snap up

111

greedily was a muzzle-loading gun. For a good one, which they judged readily enough by its chasings and other ornamentation — probably, in a word, by its contrast with a Hudson Bay trade gun — they would give astonishing prices. The finest of breech-loaders, with its finicky nonsense of shells and refilling apparatus, was despised in comparison. An old friend of my own, who possessed the only muzzle-loader I have ever fired, and who held precisely opposite views from the Indians on their merits, made a very handsome deal on such a transaction.

Individual cases of white men's insolence and injustice toward Indians were occasionally heard of on the Canadian side of the border. One of the earliest Canadian newspapers I ever saw thought it a smart thing to headline a notice of a Blood Indian discovered dead on the prairie in southern Alberta — "A Good Indian Found." But without any shred of sympathy for the smug pharisaism one sometimes hears, it is broadly true to say that the earlier spade-work of good men among the Indians had borne fruit. The general record of the Hudson's Bay Company will bear comparison with that of most trading corporations. The missionaries, followed by the Mounted Police, built a splendid tradition of strict, even-handed justice for red men as well as white. All this had inculcated in the Indian mind a general belief in fair dealing upon which they might rely.

I do not forget one or two bloody episodes, such as Charcoal in 1896 and Almighty Voice in 1897. In all likelihood we shall never know the actual origin of the occurrences or motives which culminated in them running amuck. I greatly doubt whether these men began as killers; I suspect they merely ended as such. I do not believe that any decent white man was ever in any danger from an Indian in our time.

I have never been able to witness or even to contemplate the occasional gala festivities among reservation Indians, treaty days and the like, with their gaping photographic idlers, without feeling heartsick. I have never gone to such displays deliberately. On one occasion I found myself present unintentionally. I was the guest of the missionary on Paul's Reserve at Wabamun Lake, my old friend Rev. P.G. Sutton, afterwards of Vancouver. The treaty money was paid just below the Mission House. The thought would not be quelled that these people were the original owners of this land farther back than we have any knowledge and that they had been deposed and disinherited by the good old rule, the simple plan, that they may take who have the power and they may keep who can.

I discovered on this particular occasion that so far from 'these people not minding that sort of thing', some of them resented the intrusive cameras very deeply and would not pose for them. Nor was this any magical dread. For on learning that my wife and I were the missionary's guests, she was invited to see their tepees and their babies, and her camera was at once exempted from the ban! I cannot imagine any finer tribute to a missionary's character and influence than that. No Indian was allowed to enter his predecessor's house. Why some people are missionaries at all passes understanding.

While Canada has been happily free from overt brutalities, there has been and still is plenty of bureaucratic stupidity and social caste exclusiveness. It was long ordained by a paternalistic Indian Department that at a prescribed age every Indian child must go to the residential Indian school. God alone knows why! They were taken virtually by force for this purpose; commonly against their parents' will and their own. When the years of their education were over, they could return to their prostituted caricature of their ancient life and endure the red man's hell as best they might. The only active participation in a common Canadian life is to make them a gazing-stock and a sport once a year or so. I cannot avoid contrasting this with what I have seen in Honolulu where the social elite are only too proud if they can advertise and display a native Hawaiian descent in their family or Christian names. I am given to understand that in the precise area to which I have referred, the Indian Department have at last consented after years of effort to allow the children to attend a local Indian school where they can live at home. I have never yet met a Canadian Indian school worker who is not consumed with shame and despair at the Helot-treatment. I have, however, met an Alberta pureblood Cree girl whose grandfather, father, and uncle were college trained and the first of them an outstanding Greek scholar, whose natural dignity was fortified by a pride in her pure racial (and tribal) descent, which could not possible be surpassed by any titled scion with his four-and-sixty quarterings.

This is not wholly an old man's armchair philosophy. In October 1897, I freighted two trappers and their winter's outfit into Battle Lake. This and Pigeon Lake somewhat farther north, are the joint headwaters of the Battle River. Battle Lake is between forty and fifty miles westward from Ponoka, and about seventy-five southwest of Edmonton. We kept to the Pigeon Lake trail up to Pigeon Creek ford; after crossing which we struck across country to the Battle Creek valley and followed that to the lake. The elder and leader of the two was an American who had knocked about the West very considerably. He was bluff and hearty enough in his manner towards 'equals', but never leaving one long uninformed that he was a white man. There was perhaps a logic of sorts in this for he bore no other perceptible token of superiority. He had wintered at Battle Lake two years previously and hoped to find his old shack still standing. When we reached the lake we found it still standing, certainly, but half the roof had been stripped off, which I very well remember made a bitterly cold bivouac that frosty October night, since we daren't light any fire inside in that condition. The destruction was manifestly recent, for the debris were heaped about the walls and doorway. It was apparently the work of a band of Stoneys, of whom we had heard as being at the lake and whose camp was around the end, about half a mile away. Whoever did it doubtless intended to discourage futher pre-emptions.

These Stoneys were a reservation band from the Morley Reserve, west of Calgary. They had apparently tired of reservation life and longed for a spell of the old days. It was said that they had broken out without leave but since the police knew perfectly well where they were and no complaints of their conduct had been received, the authorities winked at the irregularity. There were no settlers within thirty miles of them to make any complaints. I cannot vouch for the truth of all this, but it was the account current at the time. They had now for some months, in fact since spring, been living as their fathers did, by hunting and trapping, and as we subsequently learned, were intending to winter in their present camp. They regarded themselves — not altogether without justice — as having priority rights, and bitterly resented our intrusion. The trapper on his side, although he had no licence or official authorization of any character ("I got the Winchester, an' that's good enough for me!") was equally furious at the unroofing the shack. There was material for a first-class row.

The old chief of the band came around next morning and there was an angry altercation between him and the trapper, or rather between the trapper and the old man's younger followers. There were abundant references to "white men" and "goddam Nitchie sons o' bitches" together with much slapping and brandishing aloft of the Winchester. What interested me above all else were the two respective leaders. The old chief was a man whom I took to be of sixty years or so which took him back to about 1837, well into the old days. He was badly crippled by rheumatism or wounds, perhaps both, and had to be assisted somewhat by his younger companions. Though he could no longer stand upright, clearly there had once been a time when he could. For he had yet that native dignity which all Indian chiefs seem to have derived from somewhere, wherever it be. I have never in my life seen a man who typified more regally and utterly Shakespeare's inimitable phrase — "Every inch a king!" And as I looked at his opponent, the paltry trash about 'white man' — could look at the two and doubt for a moment who was the patrician and who the helot, the boor. Thirty years later I described the old man to the Stoney chief on Paul's Reserve, in my friend Sutton's mission house. My description (with abundant signs) was recognized at once and I learned that Sutton's friend was a boy in that camp!

Meanwhile another question loomed up. I had to return home alone with my team and wagon next day. For forty miles, to the outskirts of Ponoka, there wasn't a house and I knew I had to camp overnight on the way. I had been careful to take no part in the quarrel, which was none of my business, even had my sympathies been other than they were. But would the Stoneys respect my neutrality? Without knowing it definitely I had done the wisest thing in holding aloof. But I was not then historically aware that while some tribes did respect neutrality, others flung away such fine distinctions; the friend of their enemy was their enemy likewise. This was notably the Sioux 'political theory' and this reasoning had cost Father Aulneau and one of La Verendrye's sons their lives in 1736. I was then ignorant both of this and even of the more important fact that the Stoneys are Sioux, or were down to about 1640. The trapper thought "the red bastards wouldn't dare." I hoped not.

I made no attempt to sneak off secretly. I can imagine nothing less propitious for secrecy than a wagon at daybreak on a calm and frosty October morning, even without running the gauntlet of a hunter's ears. I was not molested. Two or three miles along the trail I met one of the chief's supporters of the previous day. Thirty years later I could at least have given him the Stoney greeting in its colloquial form — *Ambostich*. All I could do then was to point forward — "Ponoka"; the one word we had in common. We had a pleasant 'chat' made up of signs and smiles and parted good friends. British justice had done its good work and that Sunday morning I reaped the fruits. I am not altogether sure whether I could have trusted the 'white man' in similar circumstances. The Stoneys ran him out long before winter was over. He was no neutral!

Some few years later a murder was committed by an Indian in the Buffalo Lake country southeast of us. The local paper stated it was thought the murderer would make across country toward Lacombe and strike for the heavy timber territory west of Gull Lake, which could furnish cover all the way to the Arctic. One bitter Sunday morning at this precise time I had been watering the cattle at the spring and I noticed a thin smoke rising in the nearby woods on my place. I went over and found a Cree of about thirty, together with another somewhat younger, a lad of perhaps eighteen. They had a small fire ("Nitchie fashion: small fire and sit close up. White man: big fire and sit away off!"). There was a well-blackened billy-can of tea on the fire but no food in sight. They told me they were making for Lacombe across country — "shorter." Obviously it was shorter but the snow was deep, and this was January and some forty below or thereabouts that very day. They had run out of grub and had only the tea, and ten miles of heavy going over a storm-swept country staring them in the face. So I told them to come and have some hot dinner.

My mother and I were alone at this time. When I presented myself at our door with my two companions I thought at first she was going to collapse on the spot. She was quite certain (she told me later) that the tall, older Indian was the murderer and I was his prisoner and that we should end up by being slain and scalped! My laugh when I saw her consternation must have reassured her. When she heard that these were merely two starving men, she proceeded both in letter and in spirit to obey the apostolic injunction — "If thine enemy hunger, feed him. . . ." I don't think our dinner table ever saw stranger guests. There was a huge stew jar of young, tender beef with rich gravy and potatoes, cabbage, etc., followed by a pie or pudding and oceans of hot tea. And how those two fellows went after it! They certainly went on their way rejoicing. Whenever my mother or I saw that tall Cree in town after that he always came and shook hands!

I have never felt quite certain he hadn't something to do with that murder. The going across country afoot at that very time had a suspicious look; he couldn't have followed the same route on horseback without a great deal more publicity. I have forgotten whether the murderer's identity was fully known or not. Had it not been, I could quite easily have believed our guest to be the murderer himself. Since they never got the man — if I remember correctly — this is at least possible. It would moreover be getting dark as our two guests approached Lacombe. The two might also be making a conspicuously ostentatious trek across country while some friend, the real murderer, escaped much less obtrusively behind this smokescreen. I never gave any information concerning these men. There might have been provocation. I have always felt I could forgive a hot-blooded murder easier than a cold-blooded lie, for example. It seems a pretty problem, none the less.

17

Community Life

In a society so completely unorganized as was ours, it is not to be expected that organized recreational activities could be looked for. Such amenities need a recognized centre for their expression. It generally required the formal establishment of a school district to create and disseminate the inner subconscious sense of communal identity, and also to provide a common assembly hall where the practical efforts which are anticipated as its logical consequence can find a home. The school district in itself was regarded as a distinct landmark in the march of progress. "They've got a school district over there" was a very high testimonial.

In some cases I know, so far from the establishment of school districts engendering any very active sense of unity among the residents, they tended rather the other way. It frequently required a little prodding from the Department of Education to get the thing going. Some of those without children or whose families had passed out of school viewed the affair as a disagreeable expense, a thing to be blocked as long as possible. When these had been silenced if not convinced, the future site became a burning question. New districts were commonly adjoining or contiguous to existing ones, and were always of a certain maximum size so that no home should be more than so many miles from the school since its owner could then refuse to pay the school tax. As a result of this, when the foundation of a new district began to be talked of, it was not difficult to forecast very probably just wherabouts its geographical centre must be. Very much like the 'gerrymandering' which — according to the 'opposition' at least — accompanies (or motivates) redistribution campaigns, there was a considerable amount of heart (and map) searching by some astute individuals to see whether by leaving out a couple of unoccupied — or sometimes not unoccupied — sections in one direction and loud-pedalling the advisability or bare justice of including Jones with six children in another they might not bring the centre and probable school site a mile or more nearer to their own place.

Proximity to the school was both an important present asset to a man with a family (even if the Jones children walked three miles) and a valuable potential asset to a farm in event of later sales. While a really good site close to the centre might have to be bought, 'public spirited citizens' were often prepared to donate one. (Even in those days, long before the World Wars, I never remember a site being given, they were invariably 'donated'.) It has not infrequently been found that such a plot was in some completely worthless corner of his land, only to be made practicable at considerable expense and the intention of the philanthropist was quite patently to raise the value of his own place. This was enacting over again the policy of some of the ancient 'pious founders' in the Middle Ages, making the best of both worlds. As the abbey sites and the ancient charters both reveal, those men frequently gave the monks a stretch of swamp which is why the monks were often the first to introduce drainage into a region. They had to or perish.

There was frequently a long and bitter contest between the respective backers and critics of the public spirited citizen (or citizens). When the site was finally decided upon (sometimes by the intervention of the Department), the question of a teacher very often precipitated another battle. Half a dozen men knew practically the only teacher suitable "for a new district like ours." Whoever was at last selected would presumably board with the friend who proposed her. Sometimes she didn't. She might herself be a "daughter of debate, who discord still doth sow." But even without this additional *casus belli,* I knew of districts where these ancient enmities never died until some of the first generation of hot protagonists for this or that had themselves died or had moved out. Recreational unity would scarcely thrive in such an atmosphere.

Even in more genial ones the modern forms of community life had not yet appeared. There were neither

United Farmers, Community Leagues, Women's Institutes, Drama Centres, whist drives, nor bridge clubs. Nor had any form of local organized sport developed. Whatever it was we did it ourselves rather than watch somebody else do it for us, whether for pay or not. We had occasional outings together, sometimes as berry-pickings on the Blindman River or elsewhere but as economic circumstances improved we became less dependent upon the saskatoons beyond immediate fresh use and, between this and the closer settlement of the country making access more difficult, berry picking expeditions fell very much into disuse.

There were occasional basket picnics at some favourite lakeside or other beauty spot or more rarely at some individual home. Nominally these would be Methodist, Pleasant Valley, Canyon School, American (on the fourth of July), or Orangemen's (on the twelfth), but whoever cared to go was made welcome. On official holidays such as the twenty-fourth of May or the first of July (Dominion Day), such local or sectional elements met in common at convenient centres, usually not more than ten or twelve miles distant. A baseball game, chiefly noticeable for the players' lack of practice, was a familiar feature of these gatherings. Summer, however, was too strenuous a season for definitely allocated vacations or recreational periods, and such would commonly be the only outdoor games of the year, at least in the rural areas.

For reasons not of leisure but of insufficient centralized numbers, organized outdoor winter sports were little heard of in the rural districts. In later years, during locomotive journeyings in the night hours, I have frequently seen skating parties of young folks, illuminated by a huge bonfire, at places far enough away from any definite village centre simply where the ice happened to be suitable. Such things were never seen in the old days except perhaps in the larger of the small towns. We ourselves had a sufficiently convenient largish stretch of ice not far from the house. But apart from laborious clearing beyond the leisure time resources of one or two persons, it was only free from snow for possibly two or three weeks after freeze-up or after the ice would bear until the snow came. During this precise period, we had to seize every precious moment of daylight and more, very frequently working on Sundays as well, in 'mudding up' our barns and stabling (that is, plastering with mud which fell out in spring) for the winter housing of our stock. For this reason, being commonly singly handed also, I never learned to skate. It must also of course be borne in mind that in our outdoor lives there was no necessity for sport as exercise. Brush-scythes, axes, grub-hoes, ploughs and pitchforks furnished exercise in abundance.

The great pivotal feature of community recreational life at any season, although in practice confined principally to wintertime, was the dance. While public dances in the larger village halls presented a more varied and ambitious program — in which desire sometimes outran performance — the naturally restricted 'ballroom space' of the ordinary farm homes reduced their affairs in actuality to the square dance in one or two sets, as the staple effort. The presiding genius at these functions was the 'caller-off' who announced the order of the movements. This was an office to whose distinctions not everyone might aspire with any hope of attaining an approved standard of accomplishment, and — like Robert Louis Stevenson's performer on the penny whistle — where the professed learned their 'mystery' is another mystery of its own. Certain past masters, ultra-proficients possessed in generous measure of the 'gift of the gab', who like the humorous auctioneer could spice the orthodox ritual with a ready seasoning of improvised patter, bore reputations which extended for miles around and were in high demand. Curiously enough, some of these magicians 'couldn't say boo to a goose' when they shed their state and descended to the common level. The music at these festive gatherings was sometimes fearfully and wonderfully made. One could hear 'relief' executants, anxious for practice or distinction, whose time-rhythm — which after all was the vital *desideratum* — was almost perfect, but whose notes in some familiar tune ranged from China to Peru!

In respect of music, we in our own district were quite exceptionally fortunate. There were three brothers who could play almost any stringed instrument with a most extraordinary skill. The youngest of the three was an absolute master of the banjo, and possessed a most magnificent instrument. This had been brought from England by a remittance man dilettante, who would never touch it again after hearing this lad's performance. Our New York friend, who was not incompetent to judge, told us he had never heard its equal among many highly advertised professionals and I myself in later years once heard a "World's Champion Banjoist" who quite certainly did not approach it. This lad was actually interviewed by several managers or their scouts and would have been eagerly grabbed but for the fatal disqualification of being unable to read music. His own wide repertoire — which was letter perfect — had been acquired from phonograph records which had only to be heard twice.

In addition to this family, there was a small but competent 'musical set', the pupils and associates of an ancient virtuoso from England, then in process of bibulous decay. Some of these later became professional musicians and teachers. They frequently played for a friendly Anglican parson who held services at a schoolhouse which had then no instrument. One Sunday, desirous to render a new 'voluntary' and having none, and being moreover tempted of the devil they gave the introductory prelude to Albert Chevalier's well-known coster song, "My Old Dutch." Its almost weird tenderness and pathos (rendered with feeling) imposed completely upon the elect and the unregenerates kept their own counsel — for the moment. In addition to playing for a fee at the public dances at the larger centres they would, if not otherwise engaged, freely turn out and help their friends to 'make it go'.

The neighbourhood dances aroused vast enthusiasm, particularly when held at certain homes which had won a special reputation for friendliness and hospitality. People thought nothing of driving any distance from five to twenty-five miles in an open bob-sleigh, with the temperature sometimes well below zero. Stabling for teams was the only factor of importance within reasonable limits. This was not, as might be thought, a question of being reluctant to leave blanketed horses outside. It was rather that certain homes were disliked in very cold weather because the stables were actually too warm to turn horses out again in the small hours. For such reasons distant visitors would sometimes bunk down for the night. But the return home next day tired and satiated, was a weary, flat, stale and unprofitable business in comparison with the joyous anticipatory journey of the night before. It was quite decidedly 'the morning after'.

There were always some at every gathering who did not dance. Some of these were elders who were past it but did not wish to miss the fun; perhaps also girls who had (as yet) nobody else to take them. There were others also who seldom or never danced, but who were eagerly sought after to sing or recite during the lengthy supper interval, commonly regarded with manifest awe by those who could do nothing but dance and who were dumb — in both the standard and Americanese sense — the moment the fiddler stopped.

One much approved variation from the 'invitation dance' was the surprise party. This bore no resemblance beyond the name to the original form of surprise party which gave the title in New England and the Middle States where the village folk invaded the parsonage or the home of some needy neighbour with all manner of supplies for the winter, and where the surprise was a genuine thing. Ours was a mere travesty of the name. There was no surprise about it. The hosts knew perfectly that the guests were coming and when. In many cases they themselves took the intitiative in arranging the affair with those who were ostensibly 'getting it up'. By this transparent fiction, they were spared the indignity of having to ask invited guests to 'bring their own chuck' and were able — with some difficulty, one would suppose — to bring a suggestion of spontaneity to the thanks or the remonstrances with which they accepted it for the table at large.

But this expedient was something of a boomerang. It no doubt enabled poorer people (or stingier ones) to share in the joys of hospitality where the expense of a large invitation party might have been enough to shut them out. But it also deprived them of the privilege of deciding for themselves who should or should not be their guests. There were certain individuals (almost invariably 'from town') whom no careful hostess would invite. Whatever the reality might be, without the form of direct invitation, no one could technically be a gate-crasher, even if personally unwelcome. The (necessarily) less rigid process of selection made it difficult to exclude the friends of friends' friends. In the case of bachelors, such guests were not even expected to bring anything. One heard now and then of young girls having danced with "that Mr. So-and-so (a not very nice man from town)," where, without causing the open scandal that all wished to avoid, neither hostess nor parent

123

could do anything beyond warning them for future occasions. Sometimes these were themselves unaware of the true situation until afterwards. But the atmosphere, with such rare exceptions, was one of innocent and hearty enjoyment. I never heard of fathers or brothers having to resort to drastic measures.

One thing may be said. I yield to none in my admiration for the modern girl who is, I believe, preponderantly, in most respects as wholesome and lovable as ever. But whatever those of today may owe to the greater freedoms of modern athletic usages or to the arts of the beautician, their prairie mothers achieved with little aid save that of the Great Beautician, nature. Different from the hectic charmers of some modern ballrooms, they glowed in abundance with an ingrained wholesomeness such as good health, clean living, and soap and water can bestow in unsurpassed excellence.

We were never at any time keen dance-goers, for reasons which will readily be inferred by readers of these pages. Nor did we ever give a dance in our own home. My mother disliked it and we were never reduced to dancing, as some were, by reason of any povery of tastes or invention. But in addition to occasional doings in the summertime, there were always each winter the two junketings in Christmas week and in February. At these gatherings, which my mother and we were alike firm in retaining strictly as invitation parties, we had everything except dancing. In a year or two it actually became a matter of personal pride to show how attractively and how successfully we could get along without it.

Practically all the musical talent of the district, to which I have referred, was ours for the asking. Nothing except some previously arranged public engagement was ever allowed to forestall those dates. It was really remarkable — and very flattering — to note how eagerly my mother's invitations were accepted and looked forward to by some who scarcely ever went anywhere else except to dances. There were three or four really good singers of both sexes, in both classical and humorous form, together with vocal and instrumental collective effort. One at least of the company was a ready reciter, drawing at will upon Ingoldsby, Tennyson, Macaulay, Kipling, Bret Harte, and others. There were games, rough and ready charades, conundrums, punning competitions, and general jollity. And beginning with a 'formal' supper and reappearing in varied guise before the close, my mother's cunning confections, such as were not seen on every table! We never heard even the most fragmentary hint that anything was lacking through the absence of dancing. There was abundance of testimony to the contrary.

It may have been partly a repercussion from such influences that led to a not unfruitful effort in our district — not originating with ourselves — to organize some forms of recreational community activity. These were intended to be distinct from and in some measure 'corrective' of dancing, at least of dancing as the virtually undisputed ruler of the situation. One of our neighbouring school teachers, a well-read and thoroughly vivacious girl, but one to whom dancing made no appeal, broached the idea of a Debating Society. The only 'extraneous' activity then in existence, if one may describe a once-a-year occurrence in such terms, was the annual school concert. Although there was outside (adult) assistance at this function, the principal items on the programs were not outstandingly soul-satisfying to many beyond the parents — or possibly the sisters and the cousins and the aunts — of the *artistes.*

I was at first somewhat dubious concerning the debating society project but as a prominent dissenter from the 'universalist' supremacy of dancing, I could scarcely refuse to help. Actually the thing was a triumphant success from the start. And let no supercilious critic sniff at the mention of a country debating society! In addition to "them readin' fellers" at large, our zone of influence (or whatever you please to call it) was unusually fortunate in fair debater material. Our school teacher, as the exciting cause of it all, played the game superbly. We had also two ex-school principals, men of well-stored and ready minds. These at a pinch could lead either attack or reply on almost any subject reasonably within the scope of our intellectual resources and on a given 'set' topic they well understood the arts of dividing the argument in detail among their team. Looking back now after many years, our subjects were by no means contemptible. Perhaps I may add that we never once had occasion to resort to any printed *Guide to Topics for Debate.* From the first, members were encouraged to think up such for themselves.

We wasted no time on "War versus Intemperance" or "Whether men were better than women." We became historical, political, sociological, and metaphysical. We met at our local schoolhouse and our apportioned evenings, which did not include any refreshments to tempt attendance, were eagerly anticipated and drew excellent houses. These included numbers from other school districts or localities, some of whom came to 'spy out the land'. We had occasional inter-society debates. I recall one such with an organization senior in point of time to ourselves. I cannot say whether it was our strength or their weakness but we won hands down. Even on so modest a scale, for some of us it laid the foundation for at least a modicum of self-confidence in public speech.

Perhaps emboldened by the success of this bypath of intellectual effort, and again encouraged if not first instigated by our indefatigable teacher (who had, I fear, like may prophets, little honour in her own country), we broke out in another direction. Another of our residents was a skilled musician with a very considerable knowledge of musical principles. He organized an instruction class in reading music from the Sol-Fa notation. Since he chanced to be my own brother, I was induced to attend through the bitterest and stormiest winter in more than fifty years not so much from any hope — in either of us — of any astonishingly fruitful results, but on the Voltairean principle, *pour encourager les autres.* Our teacher possessed both enthusiasm and skill. He designed and executed a Modulator more comprehensive than any I have seen elsewhere in which C was exhibited comparatively in keys of sharps and flats respectively. I treasure it still.

I never attained beyond a painful pedestrian fumbling with the staff notation in which I 'read' (save the mark!) the tune I know rather than the tune I read, while its orchestral intricacies leave me gasping. But at least I acquired a something that winter which has never been forgotten, by which I can sing in the Sol-Fa practically any tune I hear; sometimes when actually hearing it for the first time. So the instructor's winter evenings were perhaps not wholly wasted. As a matter of fact, he got some very respectable four-part singing out of us before the season closed.

18

The Aftermath of 1907

The year 1906, which had been so rich in hopeful promise, hadn't quite done with me. As late as 1908, when I ceased farming, even in the splendid Red Deer district wheat was still considered very much of a gambler's crop. Some old-timers may remember that for a few years an attempt was made to popularize fall wheat stemming from an impression that the season was too short and frequently too cool for spring wheat to be successful on a large scale. 'Alberta Red' was for a space as much of a household word as 'Red Fife' had been. What turned many against it was, I believe, the too open winters of Southern Alberta. These were generally regarded as dangerous-to-fatal for a fall sown crop. Among a few experimental trials in the North, one of the best fields I ever saw had been stripped of snow and had turned to mud twice that winter (1903-1904).

Our staple crop was oats, with barley a limping second. But some of us on high locations were making efforts at spring wheat. One neighbour in particular, a poor man who had come in late and who took a homestead nobody else would look at, a very high location where frost was impossible before winter set in properly, was able to raise wheat when nobody else could. He had no need to haul it to town; people would come to his place and buy it for seed. If his farm had ever held black soil, it had long ago rolled down the hill to the bottom lands. His crops were never large, and he had so little livestock that manuring was practically out of the question but they did ripen. His land was the highest in the neighbourhood. It could even defy the Wet Years!

On what was practically the next highest (though materially lower we could see the Rockies, two hundred miles away), on a portion where the hail had not touched, I had raised some really magnificent wheat that summer of 1906. Alas! The elevators in Lacombe where we dealt wouldn't take wheat but the elevator in Red Deer, twenty-two miles away, was buying it and thither I took it. The cheque was dishonoured, and the tale of misfortune rolled on.

The winter of 1906-1907 was the longest and hardest I ever saw while we were on the farm. The intitial snow which began on November 15 lasted for seventy-two hours without a pause and covered the country some six feet deep. We did a great deal of bush work that winter, and the deep snow made teaming heavy work of it for man and beast. We preferred on principle to work in the woods in the colder weather since we could keep our tools and our hands and feet dry and comfortable all day. That winter we had no occasion to pick and choose; I doubt whether the glass rose above freezing before the middle of April. That winter we killed a steer, of which we sold one hind quarter to a neighbour; we two lads and my mother ate up the three quarters and a fat pig during the winter. Even she could not avoid the cold completely; she had to feed her fowls and house them up before we got home o' nights. Through all this we enjoyed the most perfect health as was always the case in the coldest weather. It was during the Chinooks we had to watch for flu or other similar pests.

Our wild hay land, which was on my mother's place, was well fenced. For this reason we had no occasion to fence the stacks. We followed the usual custom of some ten or twelve loads to a stack and rather than haul in too far a distance we started another stack. Consequently we had stacks dotted about here and there over the hay meadow and each one required a short branch trail of its own whenever a new stack was attacked. If practicable we liked to haul one of the stacks home completely when once we had started on it before the trail became drifted up again. We never had any occasion to ration our livestock and in the stormy spells our home corrals shrank rapidly. We would tell ourselves that the weather would let up presently; "no need to go hauling today — not fit to turn a dog out!" But sometimes it didn't let up and one just had to go! The trip was a mile and a half each way, commonly once before dinner and once after. I blanketed my horses under the harness to offset the cold waiting while I loaded my hay and I wore my heaviest coat above everything else. It was cold enough driving down there to that shelterless expanse but that was nothing compared to stripping down to ordinary working togs when I got there. The second trip was usually about sunset, and the cloudless air almost crackling, pitchforks and hay knives glittering with frost that made hands ache through two pairs of mitts! Going home if the wind faced me I could walk behind the load. The joke of it was that after declaring it. not fit to turn a dog out, one would keep at it twice a day until the entire stack was home.

There was curious country superstition among people who should have known better that one was never frozen twice on the same day. It is utterly fallacious. I have frozen my nose a dozen times in ten miles. I recall one trip facing a bitter wind where I got so tired of doing this that I finally left the thawing until we got in. That was the last time! It took me nearly half an hour to bring it back; I was afraid I might have frozen the bone which is a serious affair. My second brother, not long out from England and enjoying (in his first winter) that curious semi-immunity from frostbites not uncommon with newly arrived Old Countrymen, flatly refused to believe the thing had actually occurred in ten minutes or so. I invited him to follow mc around for another ten , this was at sunset and in that space of time it occurred twice. In a long protracted cold snap, where the new skin has no opportunity to toughen, an exposed part is gone in no time. There is at any rate no long drawn out preliminary misery. This winter temperature went as low as sixty-eight below zero. It burnt one's throat standing as an ordinary twenty-five to thirty degree below reading might have done running.

In the warm spring of 1905 all of my fall ploughing was seeded by March 31. This year of 1907 I only began on May 3 and it wasn't until around June 10 that our spring operations were completed. Some of our more reverentially inclined neighbours felt sure that our meteorological troubles could be compensated by a longer season being 'sent' but these hopes were not fulfilled. Growth was good but maturity approached with leaden feet. The summer had been unduly cool and damp. And on September 7 — a date when I four times saw whitened prairies in Alberta — our crops were again snowed under. The conditions of 1899-1900-1901 were again repeated. Crops had again to be cut one way only. This in itself was not so difficult as handling a wind-lodged crop which has fallen over in all directions being mainly a question of losing valuable time. But the conditions which necessitated this method are in themselves highly detrimental to the ripening of crops and were so in this instance. Just at a time when frosts could be fatal, the cold wet snowfall chilled the country and induced even earlier frosts. The quality of the crop was inferior for sale for feeding and quite unfit for seed. We were almost back into 1900 when for three weeks (September 23-October 12) we could journey on sleighs only and enormous icicles hung from our eaves. Like all grains when the germ has been ruined by frost, the feeding value was heavily impaired. We had to increase the food ration for our spring fat cattle; in fact we had almost literally to pump it into them to meet the time program.

I remember one repercussion of this dismal year only too keenly. Due to the straitened conditions outlined above, our anticipated liquidation — or at worst, material reduction — of our debit account in the village had perforce to wait until spring. This did not at all suit our principal creditor. In trying to explain to this man that his account was well secured and that he couldn't get blood out of a stone, I got such a tongue lashing as I had never experienced before (nor have I since) and I just had to sit there and take it. I don't know whether I 'registered' what was called in the Army 'silent mutiny' or 'silent rebellion' or the like; it was perhaps as well that the lighting in his office was not over-brilliant. My feelings on my long, dark, solitary ride home can be imagined. I don't mean to say that I ever really got near enough to suicide to even begin to think by what choice of means I would do the act which ends all other acts, but I think I saw a glimpse of a state of mind, a glimpse as though seen through a half-open door from an anteroom to the inner chamber beyond. This black fit was of course of no long duration. I was still on the sunny side of thirty and in a mile or two I was trying to scheme out some possible ways and means of meeting my troubles but I think that since then I have been somewhat less censorious concerning the 'cowardice' of the suicide; he may have been tempted above that which he was able to bear.

After that demonstration it is a pleasure to be able to record something different. One hears a lot about soulless corporations and it is quite frequently assumed almost automatically that the larger the corporation the smaller the soul. I stood in a similar relation to the Massey-Harris Corporation but with this important distinction; in their case nothing whatever had been paid on their account since the previous fall, twelve months before. I was requested to be in Lacombe on a certain day to meet their travelling representatives. I was unaware what was to be the general policy of these men but I knew quite well that I had nothing materially different to offer them from what had already been laid before my local creditor. If I had come cheque book in hand they could scarcely have been more genial. They were "conversant with my record and could assure me that my credit with the company was perfectly good." Despite my dozen years in the country I had not yet grasped the difference between the collection department and the sales department with the ceaseless agonizings for this year's sales to surpass the previous year's figures. I wondered just what effect this year's default might have on next year's credit prospects should I need credit. I found there would be no difficulty in adding to my long term engagements if necessary, even although "pay nothing down" had not yet been added formally to the current slogans of the marketplace.

This question of implements was one which I fancy some of our friends or relatives in England never did quite understand. "Must those folks over there, struggling as they are, have all those expensive implements? Our own forefathers had spades. . . ." I myself knew one or two courageous but inexperienced men who said the same thing out here. They too, until they put the matter to the test, seemed to think that about eighty per cent of it all was the desire to keep up with the Joneses. They didn't see that time was the great deciding factor in a land where the summers were tragically short for a farmer and where skilled help wasn't always to be had very easily, even if one rolled in money! And very often when we needed these new implements we needed them in a hurry. I drove my plough into a big willow root one fine morning and there was a rending crash! My three horses were too strong for the plough and had torn it almost body from soul. Time was too valuable to wait for repairs at that moment; I had to go to town and get another (and heavier) plough. The price now seems laughable but it was scarcely laughable then — twenty-six dollars. It added

131

that sum to my liabilities but nothing whatever to my assets and however considerate one's creditors might be, payment must be met some day.

Time could be a remorseless factor. I had a considerable summer fallowing project on my hands one summer and I wished to manure a big piece of it, fortunately nearest to my stable yard. This latter was so deeply tramped with packed manure that in summer one almost mired in it. No manure loaders or spreaders then! We did it the hard way, by the Armstrong process. It cost me two solid weeks before I got my Augean stable yard cleaned down to ground level. By the time my fallow was ploughed my chances of breaking any new land were nil.

But I was never caught again. From then onward through each winter I hauled the manure out each morning direct from the stables and spread it at once. In summer, half a day cleaned up the residue. The green manure was certainly not as rich a dressing the first year but next year — oh boy! And the time saved in its most precious hour compensated abundantly.

The chief net result of the hail of 1906 and the snow of 1907 was that for the second consecutive year I had to resort to what was euphemistically called 'Free' Government Seed Grain. It may be remembered that some few years back following a crop failure in Saskatchewan, a grant-in-assistance of six hundred dollars per farmer was enacted. They were less liberal in earlier years. The recipient of free seed had to give a lien against his homestead title. This embraced in practice the brief syllogism — no title, no seed — so that for 1908 I had two years' seed to pay for before I had a penny for myself.

I gave much thought to the present situation and realized that it could not go on. The only question was what to do. There was no one, however intimate, that could tell me what I ought to do. As I have suggested, this was not the first of such introspective moments. I had long before realized why we had come to Canada: to escape the spectre of poverty confronting an aging man no longer competent to repel the fiend. I was determined that if it were at all possible that should never be my lot. I was not quite like so many fellows of my age, footloose and free to go where and howsoever I would. Circumstances had made me the chief support of my mother as

I continued to be throughout her life. She and I had a much loved home which neither of us was willing to leave except for very weighty reasons.

If and when I did leave I had no wish merely to 'get a job' somewhere; all too often one of those where "I can't pay you unless Jones pays me," a mere knockabout who as the years advanced would be expected to keep pace with younger men's thews and sinews. That would be merely to exchange one form of insecurity for another, the very dilemma that had confronted my father. We were by now doing well enough to mark time and not positively fall back but I could clearly see that it would be a long hard grind before one could meet light-heartedly the demands for maintenance and renewal in machinery and so forth, without having to eat into capital resources in livestock in order to do so. I could foresee the day when a bank account would be a necessity, as modern farmers tell me it now actually is. This would follow from the outdating of taxes we should no longer be allowed to pay in labour, from the extension of the recently mooted hail insurance and other developments. Protection against hail would avail nothing if you couldn't pay the premiums at the required time.

I discussed these economic aspects very thoroughly with a chum. Through the advancing years of his father, who had taken many small jobs off his hands, he was now facing the single handed outdoor conditions that had been my lot for ten years. A single worker, however industrious and even experienced — whatever he is doing, everything else stands still during that time. Fully abreast of these considerations, I felt there was also a psychological factor to be faced: were we fit to be homesteaders at all? We were among homesteaders, but strictly speaking not of them. We were too fond of our books and of the world that is connotated by the very mention of *books* as we understood them. A certain amount of 'spare' time was an absolute necessity in order to read and carry on any form of intellectual life — the life of a homesteader precluded this. An alternative had to be found if my life was to have any meaning at all.

There was furthermore a sort of psychological impasse. My middle (married) brother, who had remained in England to complete his apprenticeship, had recently joined us in

Alberta. My mother never had a daughter and the two women fell in love with each other for life. For two years my mother had lived in paradise. They were leaving shortly for Edmonton and I could see the wrench was going to be terrific. A separation of a hundred miles would almost be worse than a thousand. Also, there was the economic debacle of 1907.

I doubt if any one of these factors taken singly would have moved me away from the farm. I like the life and the recurrence of the seasons, no two quite alike. But the cumulative effect of the three factors in combination was irresistible. I had practically decided what I meant to turn to. Other railroads, the nuclei of the present Canadian National system (but then the Grand Trunk Pacific and Canadian Northern lines respectively) had at last thrown down the gauntlet to the oppressive premier monopoly, and were hastening west by leaps and bounds. They were simply clamouring for labour. After years of men looking for jobs, jobs were now looking for men. I determined to go in for locomotive service. Of this I knew nothing. But I had heard just enough to realize that if I worked I should be paid. I knew also — or at least I felt certain — that if a man attended to business and had half a head, together with an average share of luck, he needn't worry very much about a job as long as the age limit covered him and probably a pension at the end of it all. I saw no particular reason to think that the average railroader I met could do much that I couldn't do and in addition I knew something of the notorious 'Rule G' (drinking). I was well aware that firing an engine was supposed (most particularly by writers of railroad yarns, commonly office bred) to be something immeasurably worse than the galleys, but I had always been used to hard work, and somehow the engineers had survived it. The age of many proved that. It also suggested that the dangers of a supposedly ultra-dangerous calling might possibly have been exaggerated. My mind was made up — all I needed now was the opportunity to make the move.

19

The Economics of Change: A New Move

The season of 1908, the last year in which I farmed, was almost ideal. A traditional year in which practically everything happened as it ought to happen, no drought, frost, hail, nor storms. The few neighbours outside of our own family to whom my decision to quit farming had become known, said among themselves, "Aw! Ya' won't hear no more about Frank quittin' after a year like this. . . ."

My old next door neighbour the school trustee was heard to say "Well, I'll give him a year!" The old gentleman should have known better. Any farm accumulates a mass of the smaller hand tools and garden implements in addition to the larger ones, and innumerable small conveniences of the general order described around a service station under the comprehensive term 'parts'. These when leaving are offered at farm sales in little lots. "Anybody gimme three bucks for this lot?" — or frequently given to friends as a sort of 'keepsake'. Yet to replace them costs solid money. I knew American settlers whose 'scrap pile' as they called it was one of their most jealously prized possessions, a tried and trusted resource that had got them out of jackpots innumerable. My old friend quite forgot the economic vise that held so many of us fast. He might have been free of it but I was not. Even had I wished to return (which I never did), from the moment I left I couldn't have come back — at any rate as an owner — without such capital resources as I had no hope of possessing; resources which, had I owned them at the outset, might possibly have banished the very thought of leaving.

And all this of course touched only the economic reasons. I should never have dreamed of revealing to the world at large the various considerations that made me leave farming. At the same time I can well imagine in the face of such a season as 1908 that my persistence in leaving could easily look like sheer headstrong wilfulness to those not in possession of all my reasons for moving. I was vain enough to take such expressions of opinion from competent judges as implying at least that I was as well suited on a farm as anybody else, if I chose to stay.

Actually of course I needed a good season before I could quit decently. That wearisome succession of seasons where sometimes their very excellences had struck so hard against me, had left me up to the eyes in debt, and a lot of it with no security in the world beyond credit in the real sense of the term — that is, a belief in my willingness to pay. With my good name at stake I just couldn't walk off without a word. I have always held that anybody can go anywhere once; I like to be able to go back a second time and look people in the face. I am glad to be able to say that for many years now I haven't owed a single cent to anybody in the world.

We remained on the farm just long enough to witness the very earliest beginnings — in our locality at least — of the modern changes that were in time to revolutionize farming method. I believe that 1908 was the very last year that the threshing gangs followed the earlier practice of charging so much a bushel and the farmer feeding — and if necessary, housing — the threshing crew following the machine as distinguished from the later custom of so much per bushel which covered the cost of the crew, who took entire charge and lived in their own bunk-outfit. I remember the boarding of the machine crew particularly. A breakdown occurred on the job and we had the crew for four days with never a wheel turning during that time. It wasn't the cost because the gang allowed of that in the bill, but my mother at near seventy years of age and with five or six extra hands to be fed (and the proverbially enormous appetites of a thresher to be satisfied!) was certainly glad to see them go.

One herald of the New Age certainly made its first appearance in our midst in this year 1908. This was the automobile. We had heard of the marvel and had seen pictures of it in the magazines, and some of our more widely travelled adventurers had seen them in eastern cities. Western Canada was in that state of spiritual exaltation which a good season

Threshing crew

always brought. Everybody had some money or was likely to have. Some go-getter car salesman bethought him that this was a good opportunity to cry aloud the gospel of the car. He wasn't taking any chances on the Calgary-and-Edmonton Trail between the towns. He shipped her by rail and unloaded her at the stops for the admiring natives to gaze upon. I didn't happen to see or hear this myself since I had yet another year to go before the full vision burst upon me, but I knew the man in question quite well. A big long Westerner was gaping at the car along with the crowd. The agent asked him, "How far out do you live?" "Sixteen miles" was the reply. "Take ya' out there in forty-eight minutes.". . . "Ye're goddamned right ya' won't. There ain't no guy goin' to take *me* out home in no forty-eight minutes!" Even that was only a modest 20 mph. But Mr. B. was no revolutionary.

It was not until 1909 that I actually saw my first car. We were driving into Stettler when we noticed an extraordinary wheel print or the like on the dirt trail ahead of us, like that of a bloated megalo-super cycle. Robinson Crusoe never stared at his footprint with half the awe-stricken fascination with which this mystery gripped us. Then we remembered we had heard that a contractor grading a section of a Canadian Pacific branch line through this area had a car with which he visited his different sub-camps. On our return trip we saw it about a mile off, tearing through the parklands — and with no team in front! Very shortly after the thing came through our own yard. We had an uncompleted job of fencing on our hands; he'd got into the place and couldn't find his way out. So I undertook to pilot him to the gate, and he invited me to jump in. With its enormous brass headlights, brake (and possibly gear shift) outside, and the various pre-Ford characteristics, it looked like the last word in luxury living. I can't remember when I had my next 'first ride'; I think not before 1918.

Though 1908 was our last year of cropping, strictly speaking, we had still a place to prepare for the market, my brother's homestead some twenty-five miles east of Stettler on the baldheaded plains. This was to be properly fenced and additional acreage broken. And here we got an illuminating view of the basic injustice of the fence-and-herd laws to which I have already alluded. This was a section of territory for all practical purposes destitute of timber. Yet the poor farmer was still required to fence, while the wealthier man's herds could roam at pleasure. The crux of the problem was that here there was nothing to fence with. Not only was the poor man compelled to use costly barbed wire, the question of the posts was even more acute. The scanty local resources growing occasionally along the creek bottoms were ransacked and were ridiculously inadequate. Posts (commonly of willow, the only available wood tough and resilient enough in small sizes) had to be shipped in by rail and anything down to one and a half inches in diameter qualified as a post. Here we had a distinct advantage.

My own place, the one whereon we had been living, was conveniently near to a large willow swamp. With this problem in view we had got out some seventy willow posts the previous winter, and we now shipped these to Stettler in a boxcar by rail along with various other matters. We were fortunately able to store these in a friend's yard in Stettler pending the hauling out or they wouldn't have lasted long in that post-hungry community. Getting the posts out there was something of a chore since this and other matters involved some eight round trips by wagon of fifty miles each. The trail was level and apart from a very bad quarter-mile through soft sticky 'gumbo' it was good, and our horses were in good fettle. We developed a technique of our own. We left home the evening before and carried our breakfasts with us. It was warm spring/summer weather and we blanketed our horses and turned into our own blankets in the wagon box. At daybreak we fed our horses and ourselves, and pulled out as speedily as possible. We were generally home by noon and the horses did nothing the next day. They were as tough as wire nails and didn't lose a pound of flesh.

When we came to erect that fence it was the sensation of the neighbourhood. We had been careful not to string the posts out until we were ready to stretch the wire on them, lest a worse thing befall them. In all our wire fencing we put in a post every rod, itself an unheard-of extravagance in the untimbered country. Every fourth post was a real post, some of them up to six inches in diameter, while the intermediate ones which we called only 'stakes' were often larger than their largest posts. One could live in that area for years and never suspect that willows could grow to that size!

We left there in late July en route for Edmonton, where I intended to make my future home. We already had two home lots there, purchased in the previous winter. The lumber for our anticipated home, cut by ourselves and dressed in the planing mill at Lacombe, had also to be loaded on our boxcar at the station. En route in pursuance of these errands I had occasion to call at the old homestead where we had lived so pleasantly for a dozen years. There had as yet been no prospective purchasers around. The season had been a luxuriant one. The grass around the house inside the home fence, which had been easily kept under control by our comings and goings, stood three feet high and I had to part a way through with my hands. The air inside, coming through sashless windows, bore the rank earthy smell of the woodland jungle, utterly different from the warm pleasant odours of an inhabited home. As I stepped inside three enormous garter snakes of the super-shiny unstriped black breed, such as I at least had only seen in such deserted houses, darted in panic into some secret refuge of their own. Any feelings of homesickness that might conceivably have assailed me vanished on the instant. I never wished to see the place again. Nor did I until thirty-five years later when it looked like its old self once more.

When the home plot was purchased the previous February, the main line grade of the Grand Trunk Pacific was already completed and ran within fifty yards of our property. By the time we reached there the steel had been laid and their temporary outdoor locomotive headquarters (pending the completion of the roundhouse now under construction a mile away), the place where I hoped to get a job, was only some two hundred yards distant. Before I could go job hunting, however, we had our house to run up — including the digging of two cellars, which fell to my lot — and before that could even be started we had to haul our material from the Canadian Pacific yard on the South Side. My mother arrived a week or so behind us. Her coming permitted the emancipation of the family cat from an honourable confinement in a cage, although in full view of the family activities. He had accompanied me in the freight car, but we had not hitherto dared to trust him. With my mother's arrival he at once took over and settled down unperturbed. When all this was done, my brother had to drive back to Stettler and hand over the team to a purchaser who was aching to get for three hundred and fifty dollars what had originally cost us in cash for the two and had since given eight years of splendid work.

By this time I was at liberty to try my luck; I interviewed the locomotive foreman, whom I was surprised to find so young a man. He asked me if I could shovel coal, I said that I could shovel coal right enough. The foreman then said that there might be a need for a coal shoveller before long and would keep me in mind. He also told me that they were needing men on the extra gang down at the material yard some three miles down the track. I told him that I lived close by, and didn't want any extra gang as a permanency. I then went down and got my job on the extra gang working two days laying the first roundhouse tracks at Calder Shop. About 3 a.m. of the third day, I was aroused by a hammering on the door. I sleepily descended and found the locomotive hostler from the roundhouse 'wye' wanting to know if I was "the feller wanting work." I quickly dressed and accompanied him back to the camp where I shovelled coal on engines for the remainder of the shift and departed homewards with instructions to be on hand for duty at 7 p.m. I didn't connect at the time how I came to be called so soon after the foreman had not needed anybody "for some time yet." I very soon discovered the reason; it was payday — August 18, 1909.

When I showed up for work the next night I was regularly signed on in full with all the formalities. I was also given a sort of beginner's rule book. Pretty much as it said, it contained a few simple instructions about Refusal of Duty, Rule G, and preparing myself, progressively to accept greater responsibility. So here I was, I had crossed my Rubicon.

Concerning the change itself, I was surprisingly calm. I neither regretted the move, which would have been folly itself when once effected, nor did I especially exult in it. I recognized at the onset the improved chances of economic security for which I had left the farm but on just what levels I had yet to ascertain. The intellectual compensations for which I hoped and for which I was risking so much were even more problematical than the economic factors. Altogether I think my attitude may be defined as living from day to day and not attempting to cross bridges before I came to them and leave the rest to time and fate. By now I was under no illusions about the world owing me a living, I knew I must put a stake on the board and I meant to collect a winning ticket if I could.

Mixed freight, Northern Alberta

20

Getting the Know-How

Since the Grand Trunk Pacific was as yet in a very incomplete stage of construction, its locomotive coaling operations were primitive, however effectual. When I entered the service the roundhouse was only in process of erection, and while a coaling plant might exist on the official blueprints there were yet no signs of it, and in any case the 'wye' where we were working was itself nothing but a temporary arrangement. We expected to vacate before the end of the year. All they had at this place for coaling engines was a track elevated on trestlework to about half the height of a tender as the engine stood on the lower surface-track below. The coal cars, which were ordinary boxcars, had a false barrier inside like the grain door on a grain car, which allowed the car door proper to be closed and prevented the load from being spilt.

It soon became evident that a coalman was in no danger of 'rusting away'. Until the railroad reached the Western (Alberta) coalfields, the coal we were then handling was Pennsylvania coal, a much better quality for locomotive firing but lumpy and harder to handle in getting it out of a closed car. The hardest part was clearing a space down to floor level, where one could stand without being impeded by the false door. It was impossible to use a wheelbarrow, since nobody could have wheeled one up the steep slope to the rim of the tender. Each shovelful had to be flung over the tender separately. With my being left-handed and my mate right-handed we were each able to clean up an end of the car agreeably to our own natural movements. We threw up an unceasing cloud of coal dust, although this was nothing compared with the thick mass that hung about the later coal plant where the men were dumping Alberta slack coal down a deep chute over which they had to stand at work. Ours was at any rate sufficient that although one scrubbed himself as clean as he could before going to bed in the morning, he got up at night about the colour of an old penny, leaving blankets and pillows of similar hue.

To a man who had scarcely been out of his bed three nights in his life, night work didn't come any too easy, and our nights comprised seven every week. The night shifts (which then meant twelve hours) are as a general rule much busier than the day ones. This is particularly true of the larger centres, where senior men preferred to dwell when they could, since educational and social facilities for their families were much broader. Wholesalers wanted their shipments picked up and on their way that night and similarly their incoming freight placed on their warehouse tracks for the next day. Even passenger service could not avoid a lot of night runs. A transcontinental flyer has to be somewhere at night and when the two 'opposite numbers' met on the division, about every third or fourth one, this meant that both those crews had to work seven nights a week. I knew old passenger men who had worked seven nights a week for over twenty years. When this condition occurred at one of the jungle terminals out in the sticks, older men would often prefer daylight freight. I knew cases of very junior men unable to hold work at one station transferring to another, and the only regular engine they could hold there was the midnight flyer, which they held for months and months.

But our night shift was no matter of four or five hours and then turn in. We worked the full time most nights, with a supper hour at midnight. Three nights a week we had the mixed engine which generally had a man-sized hole in her tender after twelve hours or more. Other engines would come along at all hours: trainloads of steel rail, ballast engines, and general freight. Sometimes one of them was 'falling down for steam', or derailed ('on the ground'), and wouldn't get in. Then or at any time when our work was all done, we could turn in and sleep until something pried us out. On one of these blissful occasions we slept in a nice warm boxcar till after 7 a.m. We were awakened, looking like a bunch of chimney sweeps, by a jeering day gang to whom we had been dutifully putting up the conventional yarn about not having time to catch one's breath!

Sometimes the fellow who'd been dying for steam did manage to crawl in more dead than alive. I recall one such, about 4 o'clock one morning. The night foreman said, "They want that feller right out again." We were four that morning. "Two of you clean that fire an' the other two put twelve ton o' coal on that engine right away!" Another fellow and I reached the engine first. We took one look at the fire, and dived into the coalcar without another word. We put our twelve tons on by 7 a.m. The other two luckless hounds had managed by dint of coal picks and crowbars to penetrate only three feet down a twelve foot firebox.

I was going down the main line to work one night after a deep snowfall and I fell over some obstruction on the track. The obstruction began to discuss the situation and presently proved to be a man and a brother-worker who had unmistakably been looking upon the wine when it was red. With some difficulty, for he was a heavy man, I managed to half-lead, half-support him down to the camp cars where there were fires, for he was manifestly in no condition to be left on a railway track on a cold night with trains being pushed — the deadliest contingency of all. I found when I got to the camp that the man had been thought to be accompanying some of our own gang and his failure to show up had caused a great consternation. I wondered then and since if there would have been half the rumpus if he'd not been so helplessly drunk which makes some men extraordinarily solicitous in these cases. One man, a fellow-proficient with the castaway in the alcoholic arts, who I thought would hardly have known the meaning of the word, assured me I "had his goddamned [four-letter] respect!" Altogether the popularity poll put me pretty much in the same category with the Good Shepherd of the Ninety-and-Nine, for one night at least.

The man I worked with was from Glasgow. He was the roundhouse hostler who had awakened me at 3:00 a.m. and led me to my first job on the railroad. He could do his work well enough but had great difficulty in showing me what to do and why it should be done. I have more than once been struck with the inability of such men who, while perfectly familiar with what is required to be done in a given situation, so often seemed unable to tell a novice why in order to make the objective clearer. In northern latitudes, as winter draws on, it

145

becomes necessary to let some steam flow through exposed outside pipes lest they freeze up. To a novice nothing seems so self-evidently ridiculous as a steam pipe freezing! However, let steam be fed into a pipe without an outlet whence it can escape as steam and it soon becomes a water pipe and for a water pipe to freeze is within anybody's comprehension. At the beginning all this was Greek to me. My mentor enlarged so much on the importance of not giving too much steam, without the least hint of why, that I didn't give enough steam, and consequently it condensed and froze up the water pipes on one side of a locomotive. I took care that it didn't happen again but it made me feel like a fool for several days. The haphazard resources, or lack of resources, about this temporary headquarters, with its endless coupling and uncoupling of steam pipes for what became in the roundhouse the simplest of jobs, gave me considerable insight into the hidden mysteries of hot pipe fitting of which I'd previously known nothing.

In Christmas week we moved into the new roundhouse. At this time the place was a mere shell with no floor, no water, no steam, no light and no shelter for the men. There were eighteen stalls, the concrete ramps lining the ashpits had been put in but these had not been filled up and were breast high above the natural surface. This had to be climbed with a ladder of sorts before tackling the mountainous ascent to the cab. We adopted a labour-saving technique of our own. Instead of the customary dumping of fires on the ashpit outside, which had to be shovelled away again, we put the engines into the shop 'alive' and dumped the fire in the roundhouse pits. After dowsing the hot cinders we shovelled them over into the space between one pit and the next. We soon had the first of these spaces level with the concrete breastwork; when we transferred our activities to another pit. Long before spring we had our pits filled which meant much to our comfort.

It was only now and then that I got much chance to work in the shop. It was raw enough in there, but at least one was away from the icy winds. Down at the wye we were sheltered to a great extent by the scrub but all the growth around the new shop had been cleared off and the biting breezes of a bitter January got full play. Up to this time I had never moved an engine, having been warned most emphatically against it by the Glasgow hostler; not that he cared personally about standing upon his dignity, but any casualty would be put up to him. I had been working on an engine, but had stripped that particular coalcar and wished to move her opposite the next one. This engine in the case, the 55, had sideswiped a car in a runaway episode, and her airpump had been knocked off. She had no brake and could only be stopped by throwing the reverse over and 'plugging her'. I whistled for the hostler but I learned later something was derailed and I got no reply. The engine herself was only being used as an auxiliary steam-raising service and her cab was warm and comfortable. I was nearly done and I wanted to be done. So at last I plucked up spirit to move her, brake or no brake, and just managed to 'spot her' exactly before the coal car door. I think the hostler had been hoping that I would but he wouldn't tell me to which would throw the responsibility on him. After this I did so any time there was any occasion to.

About this time I picked up a little very welcome promotion. The night foreman came out to me on the dock one bitter crackling moonlight night and told me to go into the shop and help the boiler washer. At this stage there were no hot water pumps in the shop. Boilers could only be washed out by means of the injector from a 'live' engine placed on the next track. The discharge pipe on the live engine was disconnected and a flexible hose attached. This gave the utmost pressure we could get, a rather feeble substitute for the pump but it was all we could manage. This was probably the reason for two boilers being washed out every night, to prevent mud from clogging up the fireboxes too solidly.

The boiler washer was just about ready to quit. His erstwhile assistant, my predecessor, was a big fellow from Cumberland named Joe, who had spent years as a ship's fireman over the Seven Seas. His first procedure, on learning which live engine was to be used, was to climb into her warm cab, take off his boots and go to sleep. Meanwhile the boiler washer drained off his boiler to cool down, slacked off the copper boiler plugs through which he inserted his hose, finally removing them and coupling on the flexible hose all ready for the job.

He then called to his 'helper' who should during this interval have been getting the live engine 'hot' to furnish the maximum pressure available for the improvised pump. After

147

two or three roars from the boiler washer at the top of his voice, the sleeper at last awoke, found that his fire was about at the last gasp, opened the steam blower screaming wide open enough to drain the last pound of steam from her boiler and set her flues leaking to boot, while he threw about a ton of green coal into the firebox. Following on this ritual he leaned out of the cab window to the frenzied boiler washer who had been screaming his head nearly off to make himself heard, "O.K., Mac. Whadjer want?"

Being desired to "put the gun on" he did so and promptly lay down once again; being again desired after another minute's screaming futilities to "Shut that gun off," he presently realized where he was and complied. There were even then some sixteen or twenty boiler plugs about a locomotive and at every one of these the roaring tragicomedy was re-enacted, twice at each one of them. After three or four nights of it, the poor boilerman told the foreman he could endure it no longer. He was scarcely able to speak. So Joe was transferred outside to thaw out frozen water tanks and throw switches in below zero nights while I luxuriated indoors. We did our two boilers every night, one before supper and one after, and very seldom worked after 4 a.m.

When I came on I at once got the engine hot and full of water to the brim with a good fire in her that could be stirred up at a moment's notice if needful, and the blower no more than simmering enough to keep out the smoke from the cab. He had no occasion to speak above a whisper, and I being awake never missed it once. Joe, who had had twelve or fifteen years at sea and had risen to the post of Chief Oiler, was fiercely resentful at being 'done out of his job" by a mere 'prentice but after hearing the boiler washer's report of his new helper, the foreman wouldn't reinstate him. And so ended my five month's career as a coal shoveller at the munificent wage of twenty cents an hour for an eleven hour shift.

Throughout the whole of this winter we had no lights in the shop but such as we carried about with us. The favourite was a switchman's lantern which had a guard around the globe and could be taken outside if actual switching were needed. Joe, who was somewhat indifferent, would climb on a dark engine and thrust up his lantern to look at her water gauge glass without the least regard to protruding fittings on the boiler head that no lamp guard could defy and a familiar tinkling would announce that another lamp globe had 'gone west.' After issuing eight in one week the foreman refused Joe any more, and he went around with a globeless lamp — more commonly out.

This stygian blackness had its funny side at times. I was at work one night when the customary apostolic calm was broken by successive bursts of stentorian masculine roars, punctuated by additional trills as more people (evidently) saw the joke. Not to miss this rich feast, I stumbled across precariously enough myself and found the boiler washer standing shoulder-deep in the roundhouse cesspool and blasphemously demanding aid to escape therefrom while the total personnel of the place were draped around the spot in every conceivable attitude of complete physical incapacity helpless with laughter. In fact the only person who didn't seem to be enjoying the joke was the central performer himself. His frenzied appeals for aid were almost a part of the fun. It was really some time before we could do anything.

Fortunately the abomination of desolation wasn't cold. But having said that, further palliation seems inadmissible. The cesspool was a foul content of warm grease and muddy boiler water, a disgustingly nauseous brew compounded of the super-stinks of the world. It really was a bit of a problem getting him out, he was so slippery. All his outer toggery, overalls and the like, was consigned to the scrap heap the moment we got the slimy mass peeled off him. Even the assisting staff became almost as slimily filthy as he was.

Insofar as I myself was concerned, the gods were just and of our pleasant vices made whips to scourge us. Some time later in a thick fog I fell into one of the locomotive pits myself. This could have been a bad fall onto a concrete base had I too not fallen into a foot or more of water, from which I was able to help myself out and to take immediate measures for personal safety. The hottest spot around the works was the oil car, which had to be kept at somewhere near boiling point for heavy superheated cylinder oil to be dispensable with something except an axe. This place was kept locked and I was one of those having access to the key. I locked myself in there and stripped off, firmly determined not to emerge into the below zero atmosphere until every stitch was dry. By the usual dispensation of circumstances I'd no sooner done this than oil was wanted for an outgoing locomotive, and others were awaiting my attentions at the ashpit. I remained immovably deaf to cajolery and curses alike and did not come forth until my clothes were safely dry. And as I had the only key inside with me I could defy the enemy at the gate with impunity.

Other happenings, however, might have resulted in tragedy without mitigation. Our engine tracks outside the roundhouse had been temporarily laid on the grass, pending ballasting and had tiny undulations following the original surface countours. Of these I had then no knowledge. My Glasgow friend and I were switching out a loaded car, he being on the engine. I backed him down on the car, and the first time the automatic coupling didn't 'make', a not infrequent occurrence with novices like myself. The impact drove the car back some little distance, actually without my knowing it, up a little tiny knoll which slowed it up. I stepped in to adjust the automatic 'knuckle' when something touched my shoulder. I sprang back and the same instant the car which had rolled in on me again, crashed into the tender with a concussion that in the cab would seem negligible but would certainly have been my finish had I been directly in front of it. We had three young brakemen killed almost in their first month of duty in circumstances not materially different. I never reported this episode at home.

As a result of promotions and quitters — over forty firemen quit from the System Seniority List, senior to me — I was now second-in-command in the prospective firemen's gang, and *ex officio* outside hostler in charge of engines 'beyond the ashpit'. I was not supposed as yet to put them over the turntable. While such positions are not graded formally, I had long before been made fire lighter, a responsible position since the fire lighter is answerable for seeing that an engine has water in her before being lit up and, therefore, worth a little more pay.

I was lighting up one morning when no less a man than the Chief of Motive Power came through the shop. I jumped him to learn how soon there would be a chance to go firing. He said: "You're too small. I'm only five feet six, and you're shorter than I am." My own height at that time was five feet seven and a fraction over. His figures were demonstrably false,

150

as we stood side by side. However he did not leave me totally without notice of a sort. He said, "You've got that (shop) blower on far too strong." I didn't bother to remind the excellent man that despatchers had a habit of wanting engines at very short notice. Neither did I remind him — since I didn't know it myself then — that the railroad cliche has it that the little man is very commonly ranked the best. He has to fire with his head while the brainless giant can fire with his back at a pinch. If the Chief had been in the shop a few mornings before, probably we should all have been fired on the spot. We woke up about 6:30 with a dead yard engine due to go out at 7:00. I put a hundred pounds of steam on her in twenty minutes! What official eyes don't see official hearts don't need to worry about.

My first trip firing came sooner than the Chief's wet blanket might have foretold. I had been downtown the day before when I should have been in my bed. I had done ten of my twelve hours when the foreman came in and told me to get up on the 78; she had no fireman. The train, a long double-headed mixed and way-freight, was the general supply train to the end of steel which at this time was at the Twin Bridges near Edson. I had to go just as I was in the shop in my overalls and dirt, with no time even to wash my face. We had about four hours to lose before even getting away from Edmonton. It was a scorching July day and although there were many longish intervals while we unloaded supplies for every imaginable outfit along the division — ballast camps, tie camps, bridge camps — I was on the hot sunny side of the cab and I didn't get much rest out of it. One thing I have never forgotten. My own engineer on the head engine was a fellow with a genial smile and apparently a sunny disposition yet he never offered to lift a finger to help me throughout that blistering day. The second engineer was a man of much coarser type who, until the day of his death, bore a reputation for being difficult, from which hardly a dissentient could have been found, yet towards evening he sent his fireman over to fire for me for ten miles while he himself looked after his own firing. That was a thing not easily forgotten. I was well known to both men having serviced their engines frequently during the last six months or more.

After darkness fell and I no longer had any idea whatever

151

where we were going, I did as I have always done when the going was tough; I wasted no energy in trying to guess how fast we were going or how much farther we had to go. Dog-tired as I was, I simply told myself I could put in one more fire. And in that fashion, one fire at a time, at nearly three in the morning the engineer said at last, "Well, here we are."

I got to bed in a bunk-car, and thirty seconds later somebody came to my side and said it was 7 a.m. and we were ordered for Edmonton. A later train had come in behind us, and our second engine and he would take the eastbound mixed while we had one (empty) perishable car only. This was my first experience of a conventional dispatcher's trick. Infuriated crews often wonder why one man gets the heavy train and the other man nothing instead of splitting the tonnage between the two. That would involve two trains of less-than-tonnage; by the other method the record shows one with tonnage while the no-car movement never appears on the tonnage record at all. In this way the despatching department acquires merit for a high tonnage (or approximating to tonnage) record, and everybody's happy.

We got home about 5 p.m. and I went downtown that night as it was many months since I'd had the chance. Following which I had a real sleep.

I imagine things were not yet organized on quite such a formal basis, but I never heard anything about being 'passed' for firing service. Perhaps the absence of any adverse report served as an equivalent. Years after, I was taking out an important fast freight one morning, with a young fireman whom I personally knew to be rather young at the business, a spare man like myself. He seemed somewhat tense and nervous as we were getting her ready, so I finally asked him what the trouble was. He said this was his O.K. trip for service and he wanted to make good. I said, "Good. You're O.K.'d from now on." That eased the tension, and we had a perfectly successful trip. And at the end of it I wasn't even asked for any report. Long after I had retired I learned that the younger fellows rather liked to go out with me to learn the ropes; I never rode them for being green.

I have never held greenness to be a crime if a fellow's willing to learn and has a reasonably average I.Q. I myself was the first green man hired in Edmonton by the Locomotive

Department and 'green' was assuredly no overstatement! There is one form of greennness (if you call it such) that is found in all mechanical callings. Older men introduced you to little tricks that are so simple that you wonder why you hadn't the brains to think the thing out for yourself. And then again other old men seemed to have learned nothing. It was by no means to be taken for granted when one saw a gray head sticking out of a cab window that you were looking at a Master of all the mysteries. In the days of super-steam power a younger man who had grown up on the machinery he had to handle was very frequently better than the veteran who had been 'made on teapots' and overtaken by the juggernaut class. These too had their Louis XVIII type, who had learned nothing and forgotten nothing. But even that was not a rule.

21

Railroad Days and Railroad Ways

During the next few years I got excellent opportunities of studying engineers at close range, and also of seeing how differently the same engine pulling the same load can be handled by different men. This may seem like nonsense but it is the literal truth. We had never at any time on any steam locomotive I ever handled — and this embraces every kind except a Mallet — any sort of speedometer whatever. Our mechanical devices for regulating speed were the throttle and the reversing lever. The latter was far more than a mere means for altering the engine's direction. Its notched quadrant from 'Front corner' up to Centre provided a richly flexible range of standards by which you could work your engine with the throttle as an auxiliary for modifications of power over the smaller 'humps' that did not require any definite readjustment. The ability to hit the right combination, to 'marry your tonnage and your time-card', depended upon the engineer's 'ear for music' and is really the acid test.

Once, in a hospital ward, one of our company was wondering how an engineer, due at a place at a definite time, managed to show up at the precise moment, travelling over a long division. I told him we never bothered our heads about the time we were due at the far end. We went from one station to the next, being careful not to pass the final switch ahead of time; a serious offence which could easily on a single track road be a fatal one. If you've managed this successfully from A to Y, it doesn't take very much to do it from Y to Z.

A steam locomotive, pulling out of a yard with a heavy freight starting from a dead stand and emitting the fearsome roars we have all heard, has her reverse lever 'in the front corner'. This represents maximum power, and is the equivalent of a car in low gear. Pulling it back a notch or two at a time (in accordance with the grade) to 15 mph or so means middle gear. And the shortened exhaust of a passenger flyer on the run, so soft that her trailing cloud of glory is beaten back onto the coach roofs, yet with each separate exhaust distinctly to be heard, means that the reverse is up within one notch of Centre, corresponding to high gear. If the separate exhaust cannot be heard but instead a tearing sound is coming from the stack, the engineer is working her too low; the valves are admitting more steam than can be exhausted at that speed, and she is choking herself. A notch too many at ten or twelve mph makes little difference but at forty or fifty it means the difference between a good job and murder! This is precisely what some of the 'longstrokers' have never realized.

It was the men who didn't apologize who were the heartbreakers. It is literal truth to say that some men used as much coal going one way as others would burn on the round trip. And as often as not they positively oozed conceit and would criticize the other man's way of handling the job. The reactions of the firemen were curious. One man would say, "Some s.o.b. is goin' to pay for this!" while another took it as a lesson how not to run an engine. Some of the 'butchers' were the finest mates conceivable, "share his last crust with you" or shake down your fire for you. But plenty of the 'artists' would do that just as readily, with much less need for their compassionate assistance. Personally I always felt that if the 'hoghead' handled her with due judgment I could attend to my own fire-shakings and last crusts. One old egotist apparently thought — if the company didn't — that he ought to be on passenger. He would look at his watch leaving the last water tank, with forty miles to go and four hundred feet to climb — "Well, we're due in town at . . . " And we had to be there as if we'd been pulling the President! Fifteen minutes more would have made no difference whatever to the train. More than once I put seventeen tons 'through the rathole' in five hours, and the last half of the tender had to be handled twice to bring it forward within reach of the fire door.

And then there were the artists! In local passenger service (always heavier on coal) I have come over half the division with a fire every four miles and with the boiler feed, adjusted to balance the water consumption exactly, never cut

155

off over the whole division with its twenty-three stops. This was being done every day and though nobody knows better than the fireman that it involved good firing, that good firing was itself impossible without uniformly economical driving.

I recall two men, opposite numbers on the same run, after the half-way coaling plants were installed. Some 'chisellers' would take ten tons and book five, which was fine for their records but disastrous for the poor coalman's accounts. The first of these two passenger men was a notorious 'hard hitter' who needed the coal. His daily toll ran around six or seven tons, since the engine ran through to Saskatoon. The second man, who was as thrifty as the other was wasteful, chalked up about three tons. This man had been working out of distant terminals and was a stranger to the local Superintendent of Motive Power. That gentleman sent him a 'snooty' letter concerning "his failure to co-operate with the Locomotive Department by turning in inaccurate coal records" and warning him of severe consequences unless there was a change. The Master Mechanic, who knew the second man well, warned his Chief that he was treading on thin ice but the Chief thought the fraud was too obvious. Experienced men can generally tell how much they are using but the offending 'hogger' and his fireman took the trouble to weigh a full scoop of coal, and then counted the number of scoops over the division. The result was practically identical with their daily reports. I never heard whether the M.M. seasoned the dish with any 'I told you so's' but the conclusion was that the first man got severely reproved for wastefulness. The firemen used to say there was no downhill on his divisions, it was all up! The Chief himself, once he got to know his new men, following on amalgamation, was an experienced and reasonable man to whom anybody could talk.

My first definite firing assignment (which itself was only a T.V. — i.e. temporary vacancy) came near to being disastrous. While a firing candidate will naturally be sent out from his own home station if required, yet if a call comes from some foreign point he must either obey this or be dismissed for refusal of duty. Nobody told us that by reserving the right to return there when seniority conditions permitted me to work from there (as I later on insisted upon doing as a spare engineer under identical conditions) this right would be respected. As it was I found that my involuntary obedience to orders was classed as a 'transfer' to Edson; and I could only return home under very complicated rules set forth in the Firemen's Schedule, involving long delay and the maintaining of two homes. Of all this I suspected nothing.

I was destined for the tracklayer of the 'pioneer' as we called it, whose fireman (one of two) had fallen sick. This machine was an ingenious aggregation of cunning devices for the handling of heavy ties and half-ton rails with as little human effort as possible. It has no boiler power of its own but was pushed by two locomotives. The front locomotive furnished steam to the pioneer, while the second — which was requiring my services — pushed/pulled the train. The train itself consisted of cars carrying enough material to lay a mile of track, followed by the commissary, cooking, dining, and bunk cars of the tracklaying gang so that in case of any breakdown or delay they had their home and chuck close at hand. We were near to Jasper, into which place steel was laid that week, and in the heart of the Rockies which I had never seen before.

In order to preclude the tracklayer (the Sacred Cow of the enterprise) from being tied up, each locomotive was manned by three men: engineer, fireman and watchman. By arrangements satisfactory to themselves, or at any rate to the engineer, they divided the work among the three so that two of them could man the engine for twenty-four hours if necessary and her workday was seldom less. While the pioneer was actually at work she only moved forward a rail length, then thirty-six feet, at once and while enough track was being spaced and spiked for this, there was time for the engineman to throw in a fire or work the injector. Through the day some form of the triple combination kept the works moving, mainly the fireman in order to give the engineer and watchman as much rest as possible for the duties of the night. After the pioneer had been disconnected and supper was over, their heavy duty session began. The empty material cars had to be switched out of the train, and next day's loads of ties and steel to be 'cut in' in their place. The two engines had then to be taken — sometimes several miles — together with their water cars and camp water tanks to some suitable creek or lake with fit water for boiler and domestic use, and siphoned full for the next day's needs. On their return they must be spotted at the coal car while their fires were cleaned and ashpans hoed out by their respective watchmen. And so another day was ushered in.

Tracklayer - 'Pioneer'

The three enginemen had all to be of a self-reliant type, who could be expected to deal with minor contingencies in their several fields without needing to dig some bone-weary fellow out of bed for a mere nothing. Most particularly the engineer needed to be a resourceful fellow who could keep his engine working until her next regular visit to the shop. He had of course a blacksmith shop, a machine shop, and 'parts' galore to draw upon; and if all these immediate resources failed and he had to phone in to the terminal shop for some vital feature, it had better be on its way that same night or numerous V.I.P.s from China to Peru would be demanding to know WHY?? — and not in noticeably conciliatory language either. Never mind if the enginemen did draw twenty-five hours a day 'straight time', plus half an hour's 'preparatory time', and the same 'inspection time'. Anything went so long as the pioneer wasn't standing still! Even labour organizers won victories that astonished themselves by the mere mention of this supreme menace.

It was after the tracklayer had shut down for the winter that I found myself faced by the chilling ultimatum I have mentioned: I had 'transferred' to Edson. Coupled with the knockabout starvation existence of a spare fireman at a lean jungle terminal, with a trip a week, meals at the station 'beanery' on 'pie tickets', and for a home a bunkhouse where the only books were Rule Books, railroading the only intelligible topic of conversation, and gambling the only social diversion, the prospect was not appealing. When the Chief Despatcher, an ancient veteran probably as utterly bored as we were, suggested we should all write the Rules in readiness for later needs, I for one jumped at the chance.

I recall one trip exactly at the New Year, which is now merely run-of-the-mill but might easily have been more terribly dramatic. This engineer — one never caught the same fellow twice — was a youngish man off the New York Central; a prince when sober and, so far as treatment of his fireman was concerned, no different when drunk but in relation to the public he flung caution to the winds. This night we had the West Mixed, the only sort of resemblance to passenger service, and we were 'loaded for bear'. Through this mountain division there were several longish sections where fills of varying heights would be required over stretches of sunken rock whenever the Engineering Department could locate the necessary gravel. Meanwhile skeleton trestlework had been built up to grade, to be filled in later from above — the common procedure. There were standing slow orders of ten miles an hour on such places since any emergency stop from a broken brake hose or the like could wreck train and bridge in one common ruin and with fire as an inevitable consequence since we had a gasoline car on the train. Our speed-happy engineer tore over these danger spots at what mph he happened to be making when he struck them. We heard afterward that men were cursing and women were praying in the coaches and that the crew stood guard by the conductor's valve lest any panicky passenger should attempt an unauthorized interference which would have been virtually suicidal. The firemen hated to see him go but it was the last train he ever pulled on our road.

I made my escape from this loathsome exile by a lucky chance. There was a certain fireman working out of Edmonton under conditions exactly parallel to my own, apart from the having two homes to keep. His own home territory, where he had served his probation and where his friends were, was around Edson and Jasper. He disliked the Edmonton division, which he considered too hilly though it had no parallel to the thirty-five miles' unbroken stretch that faced the firemen on the west end out of Edson. In addition to this — and most probably the real point — he wasn't getting on any too well with his engineer and this implied ultimately, with the locomotive foreman at Edmonton. He came to me on the quiet and asked if I had any objection to swapping jobs with him and working out of Edmonton. My heart leaped at the prospect but I was careful to disguise this under the fair condescension which didn't mind doing him a ·favour so long as the locomotive foreman at Edmonton was agreeable and whose consent, howsoever formal, was a formal feature in such arrangements. I learned later on that that officer was only too glad to see the back of him. So on his next trip up he brought with him the official approval of the transfer; a thing which would have been impossible later under more rigidly defined rules.

If ever a fireman's heart sang as he prepared his engine

for the homebound trip I was that man. Nobody at home had the least idea of any such change. Any trip homeward would have been good, this was glorious; and I soon found that my new engineer knew how to handle her on the hills. We did encounter one blood chilling experience which I may mention, since nothing of the sort ever occurred to me again. Just after dark we were swinging around the curves along the winding shores of Wabamun Lake, when we found ourselves staring a headlight full in the face. My mate was just on the point of 'putting her in the big hole' (i.e. giving her the emergency brake) when we swung around another bend and it vanished; we had been looking at the newly risen full moon. When I reached home at a latish hour I was met by the inquiry which by now had become stereotyped — "How long are you home for this time?" My mother's delight at my answer can be conceived.

My brother-fireman, he of the exchange, had a somewhat chequered career. About a year later he came in one morning with a very sick engineer who had to be carried from the engine to the hospital. Instead of taking extra care to see that the engine was left properly on the ashpit, that is, with abundance of water in the boiler to counteract on a hot fire, this man got off like a fellow without a care in the world. Her crown-sheet got hot and blew up, fortunately without any fatalities, but entailing the (temporary) dismissal of her engineer, who emerged from the hospital without a job. The delinquent fireman disappeared. About that very time he had a fair little pot of money left him in England, said to be some twenty-five thousand dollars, enough to help things along a bit, but scarcely sufficient for a lifetime of leisured ease to one girt about by an avid cohort of friends in need. Purple and linen were not wanting. He was wont to hang around the passenger station, resplendent in gray suit, tan shoes, and panama hat; making derogatory criticisms of boneheads who didn't know enough to get off a job like that! Then we lost sight of him.

Some twelve or more years later, I was rolling through a junction yard pulling a fast freight, and a fireman was getting an engine ready for the road. My fireman asked me if I knew that fellow. I did not. "That's —," was his reply. The man had been several turns ahead of me on our own seniority list. In the intervening years I had run the gamut from spare board work to senior fireman on crack passenger flyers and had eight or nine years engineers' rights. He had just arrrived at the point where he could hold a regular freight engine — firing!

At Edmonton I had to work my way up again by such jobs as I could hold, but this was more than balanced by being able once more to live a normal life at home. In the course of things I caught a lengthy temporary vacancy on way-freight. This decided me that for so long as freight firing was to be my portion it would be way-freight for choice. Many of the lads preferred what was termed 'chain-gang freight', officially designated through-freight. This traffic ran, in theory, as nearly non-stop to the divisional terminal as conditions admitted, but conditions didn't always admit. It was handled by as many — or as few — crews as were considered to be adequate for the work. These men were on a roster of their own and were called in regular rotation, first in and first out, regardless of their actual seniority which only operated in matters considered preferential. Chain-gang crews worked at all hours, Sundays and weekdays alike. Many men liked this as it gave them a chance to be off at different hours of the day. But they had to get their sleep and their meals as best they could and when busy or in other contingencies they might be called upon to turn round without rest. Some engineers were ruthless in demanding such turns from their own firemen; I have myself done four divisions consecutively in some thirty-six hours, well over five hundred miles. On the track layer I have never had my overalls off for a week but we were not continuously travelling.

Way-freight was a complete contrast to this. They did the station switching along the road and unloaded less than carload freight at the stations. They were the charwomen and chore boys of the division. Usually they left at 7 a.m. and got in when it happened. But — they had their meals at proper times and if many of their nights were short ones they were in bed in the small hours where a working man ought to be. And when Saturday night came, as it did sooner or later, they didn't have to lick any locomotive foreman's boots for a trip off; they walked away as if they owned the road! Several of my brother-firemen wondered what I saw in 'that slaving life' when I could hold a through-freight engine and 'scoop her over the road'.

But others told me they were generally tired when they went out; and I know that as we got older I was standing up to it as well as any, and a good deal better than some.

As soon as I could hold this particular way-freight run by assignment (i.e. against all comers) I seized on it. I found I had come at a somewhat inauspicious moment. The old engineer stood very high on the seniority list and had been in passenger service since its inauguration on the road. But alas! The old man owned a farm on which he lived, four miles out of Wainwright. The 'farming hogheads' were unpopular as a type. Too often they were 'one-track minds', good for only one thing at once and the farm came first! He'd be mentally summer fallowing or branding calves when he should have been on his job. He wouldn't 'trim her' as he should with a long hill staring him in the face — and there were plenty on his division and he'd drop down to 20 mph getting over it, and run down the other side at ninety to make it up. This is simply infuriating to a good fireman. It ruins his fire and makes the job a little hell. Some good men got so utterly disgusted that they wouldn't lift a finger to bring him back to this world. He did this one day when the General Superintendent had his private car hitched on the tail end — a man who abominated picking up speed down hills. When Old John appeared for Number Two next trip he found he'd been pulled out of passenger till further notice. He had to take a way-freight.

Working up to way-freight is one thing; dropping down to it is quite another. Old John's disgruntled ways had just lost him a favourite fireman who had voluntarily left him for something better and therefore couldn't go back; this is how I got the run. At first the old man tried 'hammering the stack' off the engine to drive me off her. However, by this time I could argue technicalities as well as he could, no great feat, and demonstrate my competence on the scoop shovel. After a bitter row in which I threatened to call in the Master Mechanic if he drove me to it, we shook hands and became fast friends. Instead of allowing the old fellow to 'hang himself' while he was doing his seat-box farming, I would rouse him up — none too gently — and put him back on the rails again. During the two years I fired with him there were no more of the bloomers that had ditched him out of his passenger run and after three years of this undignified probation his passenger rights were restored to him.

Many of the firemen looked forward with real apprehension to the final exam for promotion. To do the company justice, they made no attempt to add anything to its terrors. That type of examiner whose first duty is to prevent you passing, if it can be managed, had no place here. The boot was on the other foot. If the examiner was some old veteran who had watched the young fellow's performance as a fireman during a number of years there was almost always a genuine desire to see him get through successfully. It was always a truism on railroads at large that a man made on his own road was the best material of all.

The question docket was not a light one in the old steam days. There were some five hundred questions on the locomotive itself; this included steam distribution, breakdowns, air brake and auxiliary appliances. There were also a thousand or so questions on the Standard Rules. These all had to be answered but within reason there was no time limit to the examination. The questions were presented in a book with the answers being written beneath each question. The book was kept as a permanent record and in the event of any machinery casualty tending to throw doubt on the employee's competence, the book was examined as evidence. So far from laying any traps for the poorly equipped candidate, it was a standard procedure to have them write down any really long and tricky answers on a separate sheet for the examiner's criticism and copy them into the book after he had passed them.

As may well be imagined, there were problems with this type of examination. I knew one man, a good fireman, who refused to study for the examination at all with predictable results. The examiner had to turn him back for another six months before he could try agian; he at least learned one thing from his failed examination, studied, and passed the second time. A second failure or refusal to sit was final and the unlucky one became a brakeman.

Very different treatment was accorded to experienced engineers from other systems. The examiner, very often a fellow member of the 'Big E', the Engineers Brotherhood, could use much more discretion. However hesitant about some of the questions, everybody knew these men could go out and 'cut the mustard'. One such 'boomer' faced with the awful requirement, "Trace the air through the distributing valve," answered that "the fellow who could do that could trace a snake through South America" and was only just stopped in time from making that his written answer although the engineer-brother openly agreed with him. Copying or open oral assistance was forbidden. However, it sometimes became unavoidable at such tense moments for the examiner to have to step out for a short while ("Gee! I'm out of tobacco!"), and on his return the problem required no further attention.

Some of those 'boomers' were really wonderful men who knew every move in the game. They could look anybody in the face and talk to him, and were utterly imperturbable in any crisis. Temperamentally these men were Westerners; ancestrally some were far removed from this attribute and what could have started them 'booming' was hard to imagine. One for whom I fired, named Mason, came from New Hampshire and could have been Longfellow's village blacksmith. He had twenty-nine sevice letters from as many railroads and obviously could never have held a preference run in his entire careeer. He had a grown-up daughter whom he scarcely knew. Over the years I have often wondered what men like Mason were seeking in their wanderings. Perhaps they were simply running from something — we shall never know.

22

Tricks of the Trade

As I grew older in the service and, so to say, more instinctively conversant with the rules by the very best method of learning them, that is to say by having to observe them in everyday practice, one's capacity for humorous enjoyment of misunderstanding and misuse widened. When a bunch of fellows were laughing over some big joke in this relation it was no longer necessary to ask some older man or else miss the point. As I have hinted above, one of our keenest enjoyments was to see some junior or 'office bred' official lay a trap for himself through sheer inexperience, or, better still, fall into one of his own devising.

The absent-minded 'seat-box farming' which had cost Old John his preference passenger run had not been cured by that catastrophe. He had 'taken the hole' one day for a superior train at a hill siding that was protected against cars running down the hill by a device called a 'derail'. The derail lay on top of the rail and was designed to divert the car wheel into the ditch away from the main line. The siding was a long one with the derail at the bottom end. At this time there was no lever attached to the derail so that the switchman might make an emergency jump at the last moment and throw it on or off as might be wished. The train had to be stopped while it was lifted on or off. On this occasion the brakeman rode the front pilot to be ready for this purpose. Old John chugged easily down towards the derail but showed no signs of stopping. Realizing the situation at last the brakeman gave a terrific roar and jumped off the pilot. This brought Old John to his senses. He jammed on the emergency brake there and then. At that slow speed she could stop on a nickel — and did — with the derail right under her pilot. It so chanced that the Divisional

Superintendent's private car was on the hind end that day with his wife as a passenger therein.

The brake action of a burst airhose or a 'kicker', a dirty, sticky triple valve, is exactly identical with that of a brake deliberately set in 'emergency'. Old John knew all the tricks; the carelessness with which he fell into these silly jackpots was only equalled by the adroit way in which he squirmed his way out of them. He dropped down from the cab and started back to meet his enraged superior who was making for the head end with blood in his eye. "What's the meaning of this?" (or words to that effect). Old John stammered, "I-I-I'm not responsible for a k-k-kicker, am I Mr. — ?" The super did know that an engineer wasn't. "Oh, so that was the trouble! You should see my car. Have you cut that triple out?" Old John had cut it out; his voice almost broke in brotherly sympathy for his afflicted officer. The afflicted officer didn't ask to be shown the car with its brakes cut out, nor did he walk forward to note the derail only about two inches short of lifting the engine's forward truck-wheel off the track. Had it been the General Superintendent the Old Man would have walked around the works and read the riddle at a glance. The train crew pried the derail clear from under the pilot without having to back up and give the game away. From the vindictiveness with which the super chased Old John for years after, I suspect that the divisional super told the affair to someone, the General Superintendent or another, who asked him the question he ought to have put to the engineer. To have asked them later would have been to expose himself as he was probably warned.

His gullibility on this occasion is the more surprising since he had been badly fooled over an (imaginary) burst air hose not many months before shortly after he had been promoted to trainmaster. In construction time, before matters got organized, there was a section in the Schedule regarding terminal delay before leaving. Any delay less than thirty minutes was not paid anything; over thirty minutes the entire delay was paid for. On this occasion they were all ready to go but for some late freight. Time began to draw ominously on, fifteen minutes, then twenty. The head end brakeman was a long, American boomer with a hillbilly drawl. He asked the recently promoted young engineer if he had a big Stilson wrench in his tool bag. The lad, proud of his kit of tools, produced one whereupon the brakeman disappeared for a few minutes. Meanwhile the minutes were slipping by with the impatient super consulting his watch ever and anon to see if they could get out of the terminal without paying for the delay. At last they got the highball at 7:28, eagerly relayed forward by the triumphant super, reluctantly to be obeyed by the disgusted crew. They had got up to about ten mph when the boomer stepped across the cab and slammed the engineer's brake into emergency and at the same moment disappeared from the cab. The youthful engineer was vainly wondering what line of baloney he could think up to explain the situation when the boomer emerged from between the cars with a big Stilson and a brake hose under his arm just as the super reached that point. There was a brief dialogue between the two. Then the boomer called up: "How's your air now, hogger? O.K.?" "Let's go then," said the super with yet another look at his watch, now alas 7:50 or so! The boomer came back to the cab with the Stilson. "What did he say?" asked the hogger. "Said if it had to happen this was the best place so that's that. Anyhow," the boomer continued, "I don't mind a little delay but I sure as hell want to get paid for it." This cool hand had disconnected the air hose from the front end of the engine as evidence that he had actually had to change a hose in place of a fractured one. Here again the General Superintendent would have annexed that hose and had it tested on the shop rack with results too dreadful to contemplate.

Nearly thirty years later, when I myself was becoming something of a veteran and this Nemesis was now a vice-president of something in a hurry, I had come down from Calder Yard to take his private car off Number One and put it on a fast freight. His first reaction was a complaint at the time we'd taken to come down from Calder (backing up very strictly at fifteen mph). His next was a verbal request for me to run ahead of Number One over to Calder, some four miles, although we were now actually 'on her time', that is, she was due to leave within less than ten minutes. This was a dismissal offence, had cost men their jobs and was considered ethically wrong by most engineers. Furthermore, he had abundant time in which to obtain a written train order authorizing the train movement. A verbal request was dangerous and furnished me no protection whatever. I therefore respectfully declined to make this move without a written train order to the horror of my co-workers who were the first to denounce him. I knew where I stood; the Standard train rules were part of the law of Canada and I was prepared to defend my rights over anyone who wished me to break them. Of course, I heard no more about my refusal.

Some of the lower ranking officials had a cheerful habit of issuing quasi-official instructions to ignore Rules between stated points in the interests of efficiency; very often these Rules were safety rules. These instructions were left in the men's Bulletin Book just long enough to get the men familiar with them and after a few days would mysteriously disappear. If some traffic casualty occured in these connections the men would plead the bulletin in defence. Being challenged to produce it, it could not be found. Its existence would be denied by the prosecution and the delinquent's case lost by default, corroboration by other employees being rejected. In discussing this problem I suggested they should take a leaf out of the enemy's book, abstract the thing themselves and file it in their trade union Lodge records in readiness for a rainy day. This suggestion got nowhere and we continued to suffer from this juggling of rules.

There were other contingencies involving risks or the possibility of such in the very nature of the case without any official intervention. One such was the prime importance of being sure of the identity of the train you were required to meet at a given point. The engine number was illuminated at night but wind, smoke and storm could obscure the entire number or simply part of it. This later case could be even more dangerous. For example, there was once a bad wreck in Winnipeg yard where 'Extra 313' had orders over some opposing train. The later train crew saw Extra 213 pull into the yard but only saw the '-13', the other figure being obscured by dirt and smoke. She went out and met the real Extra 313 head on with fatal results. We had a similar problem in Edmonton one winter: we had the 2548, 2648, 2748, and 5148 all working out of the same terminal. We recognized the stern necessity of seeing something more than '48' on an engine number when she went by thus happily escaping any catastrophe.

My own worst near-accident was one of those that can

Frank Roe (nearest cab) and Grand Trunk Pacific locomotive.

happen in spite of gods and men. I was firing a local passenger leaving Wainwright at 4 p.m. Almost every day we met a heavy freight two stations out and to facilitate movement the despatcher would put us in the siding while the drag, the freight, held the main line. This December evening we followed this arrangement. We pulled up the passing track, did our station work, and went up the west switch ready to go when the freight passed. The section foreman rode up on our pilot to light the switch signal lamps. He lit them up duly and then, to our horror, opened the switch to let us out onto the main line. We roared and gesticulated but muffled in his winter clothing he never heard us. I leaped down in the desperate hope of reaching the switch before the freight came along the winding canyon. If she hit the open switch and turned over she would kill three men at least; if she didn't turn over and came down our track she would grind our wooden coaches to matchwood. At this awful moment the freight engineer whistled down the canyon. The section foreman realized the situation; he threw and locked the switch, panic stricken but safe, with the freight looming up around the curve some six car lengths away. My mate and myself, almost sick with horror, vowed that never again would any section foreman or anyone else ride the pilot on such an errand. We would have him in the cab where the situation could be clearly explained and as clearly understood.

On almost the very same spot we narrowly escaped what could have been a fatality. This was a dangerous locality; the track followed the course of a winding coulee leading down from the high prairie level to the Big Bridge over the Battle River. I knew every twist on the division and had always made it a habit to do any firing when the curve was on the engineer's side. This particular day we were on a fast train running late and picking up time. Normally we were due there about 11:10 a.m. This day it was between 4:30 and 5 p.m. and just about the time when the section crew would be quitting work. At this date the foremen were not required to carry standard watches, as was enacted the next year, and in any case we were not on time. I therefore paid particular attention around any curves since around those hills we might perhaps be seen before we could be heard.

As we swung onto a little tangent of some three hundred

yards there was the section crew frantically striving to lift their handcar clear of the track. My engineer couldn't see them so I yelled "Soak her! Handcar!" He was a cranky, ill-natured little hound, notorious over the system, so he waited till he could see for himself. Instead of an 'emergency' stop he gave an 'application' stop. The section crew were understandably panic stricken; two men were trying to lift their car over the rail while two others were attempting to push it across to clear the rail. We bore down on them with scarcely diminished speed. They jumped aside to save themselves and we sent the handcar flying into the ditch and were a train length beyond it when we stopped. We had damaged nothing on the engine except our brake hose between engine and tender which we repaired in a moment. Running late as we were the few extra minutes were of no consequence and fortunately no one was hurt.

The requisition for a new handcar brought out the salient facts but what the engineer said on the matter he never condescended to tell me. I heard something from outside sources about the danger of smashing crockery in dining cars through emergency applications of the brakes. I had twice before been in similar situations with other, more experienced engineers and they had responded instantly with the required emergency applications holding, as I did, that broken crockery was of no importance as compared to human injuries. One thing was noticeable with this engineer though, he was most pleasant to me for quite a period of time after this incident. I gathered he was expecting me to lie in order to save his job in case of any official question concerning his conduct.

23

Field Tactics

Insofar as everyday life on the railroad was concerned, it may I think be very fairly summed up in a sentence: if the weather was good the job was good; if the weather was rotten the job was rotten. This was the case for outside workers at any rate. I suspect that some such distinction has held good ever since public transportation in the more extreme climates has existed in any form. Railroading also has problems belonging to its own order. Even in areas that are classed loosely as being identical in their climatic conditions, e.g. the prairie territories in winter, vary widely in many features and a knowledge of any one locality is far from knowledge of all. For a region having a cold winter at all, the Edmonton district is one of the easiest of all in the West. True blizzards, that is, the real snow siroccos, were virtually unknown until the later eras of large scale mass clearing which gave the winds free scope. I have seen the snow plough never once leave its siding in the yard for three successive winters. Though almost all my freight firing had been done on the open plains division on the east end, when I was sent down to the baldheaded country in Saskatchewan and western Manitoba, I found that I scarcely knew what snow meant, but I was soon to learn. I found myself stationed at Biggar, Saskatchewan.

The mainline had one advantage: it lay broadly in the direction of the prevailing winds, northwest and southeast, and hence did not blow up and drift quite so deeply and persistently as the branch lines, which laid roughly across the winds. But that very factor made the despatchers very often reluctant to order out the snow ploughs until they were satisfied that the crisis was a real one, by which time the crews out on the road might be buried to the eyes. On my very first (night) trip over the division with a forty-mile blizzard blowing, I ran into snow in a slight cut, not deep enough to stall me but packed hard enough by the wind that a huge 'brick' of it smashed in my front window and almost buried me where I sat.

We were only seven miles from where we meant to have supper while our coal was being shovelled ahead so I tried to push on for there where we thought we might fit up a jury-rig for our broken window. However, before we could have made it the front of our cab would have been packed with snow and the reverse lever would have been inaccessible so we had to rip the back curtain from the cab frame where it was intended to furnish some slight protection to the fireman as he fed the fire. We rammed and stuffed it into the gap in the front window, but being no longer able to look through the front window, I had to keep my side window open all the time, which did not add to our comfort. Later on after our supper pause, we ran into the lower and rather more sheltered country and finally reached Wainwright. I booked a new pane of glass for the front window — "Very important!"

I was called the next afternoon for 'First Number Two', first section of the Coast Flyer; a train I should not have been allowed to pull out of the home terminal, never having pulled passenger before, but here at the 'turn-around' end there was nobody else to use. Incidentally my window had not been repaired: the foreman had either no glass or declined to use it on a 'foreign' engine. They had nailed the canvas on tightly but my only lookout was through my side window. The blizzard was storming away harder than ever. I knew my window would freeze hard either open or shut, so I decided that freezing open was the safer course of the two. The westward trip had been my first over the division. I had to 'whistle my green' to all trains and get their answers. And since I didn't know whether the approaches to this or that station were around curves or on the straight, or uphill or down dale, while the very fences and telegraph poles were invisible, I didn't dare to miss the mileboards — "One Mile to..." Once I encountered this I disregarded the timetable completely. I slowed down to an easy gait to be able to stop on the instant if the circumstance should require it. I don't think my face was dry during the whole hundred and forty miles. When we were still some twenty-five miles short of the terminal we struck a snowbank

174

that almost buried us, and put out all my lights. It says something for my ignorance of real snow that I didn't even know the actual cause of this. The dynamo, which was on the boiler immediately ahead of the cab, should have had a protective over-shield ahead of it to meet such conditions. Later I found the older heads tying a sack or a canvas over the dynamo to preclude such accidents. As it was, the packed snow had got under the dynamo brushes and destroyed all friction.

There being no other course open I simply kept on going, making lots of noise to atone for having no lights. Fortunately there was virtually no highway traffic about on such a day. I had a junction and a registry office to negotiate but here the operator, knowing who I was, very obligingly became a co-operator and gave me a clear signal without my asking. As I approached the final terminal yard I slowed down; my brakeman put two red fuses, the only ones we had, on the front end and behind this display of fireworks we came safely into town. I was twenty minutes late. I explained the circumstances in my Late Report, but I never heard another word about it, not even the clear illegality of running totally without a headlight. I brought First Number Two into town in one piece and that was all they cared about. I pulled her again next trip.

I was called one bitterly cold February morning for a 3:30 a.m. snow plough over the Battleford branch to clear the road out for the regular Mixed. All services over this division were supposed to be equipped with an auxiliary water car, since there was no water tank for the entire sixty-five mile division. On this occasion — with a complete stranger to the road — there was no water car available! I was told, however, by way of tempering the wind to the shorn lamb, that the last eighteen miles into Battleford were all downhill, and "she'll drift." Probably in summer she might.

Snow plough service is the most loathed and dreaded of all forms of locomotive duty. The engineer has no chance to see where he is going, and yet he is held responsible. The operation of the plough is controlled by the man riding in the plough's 'cupola', generally the roadmaster or some senior section foreman. He communicates his wishes by an official code of signals operating through the engine's air signal line, connected up between the snow plough and the cab, the signals being those used by the same apparatus in passenger service.

As already explained, this branch ran roughly at right angles to the two prevailing winds (NW and SE) and was badly blocked. Very frequently we had to back up and take a second rush at a deepish cut, an additional strain upon our meagre water supply but worse was to follow. Our compressed air system (designed far to the south!) had abundant provision for cooling the ninety pound high pressure air, but none for preventing this cooling. The return pipes — hot at first — became partly cemented with ice from the blocks of hard snow thrown out by the plough and soon were unable to deliver compressed air to the plough at anything like the pressure required to spread the plough 'wings' wide enough to make a serviceable job of clearing the cuts along the track. After this fashion we at last reached a point which I was told was only five miles from the tank but in a temperature of forty-five below zero and the rail covered with gritty snow that ground under her drivers, she utterly refused to 'drift'. We were down so low for water that I in my turn refused to work steam down the hill lest I found myself completely run dry and not yet at the tank and I couldn't run down 'light engine' because I had the plough outfit in front of me. So I decided to wait until the Mixed overtook us and could push me down to the tank.

We tried shovelling snow into our tender, hoping to melt it with steam from our injectors but this was insufficient for that purpose and we had no large size steam hose with us. Although the blocks of snow looked clean enough, there was enough grass in them to partly block our hose-bag strainers, as we discovered later on. Presently the Mixed came along and pushed us down to the water tank and that phase of our troubles passed on into the limbo of forgotten things.

Then a further complication arose. The engine off the Mixed, duly replete with water car, was ordered to take on the snow plough for another eighty miles or so while we were to take the Mixed back to Biggar. I had only the veriest whisper of air left on my engine, just enough to handle the engine without any cars. But the Mixed had a passenger coach on and came under the regulations governing, not 'passenger trains', but "all trains carrying passengers" — which rendered juggling or evasions more difficult. I called up the despatcher and explained my situation, stating that I could bring her in as I was. To this he made no reply whatever. If he'd ordered me to do so the responsibility would be his. If he ordered me not to do so the responsibility for leaving the public stranded out there in the country would be his again. He declined to shoulder either burden.

I discussed the predicament with the conductor, and asked him not to couple the air brakes on the train as I could handle things better if I had a little air for the engine and also because there were some cars to switch at the elevators on our way down. He agreed not to but either he or his brakeman, through sheer habit or else deliberately, coupled in the air as usual when the engine was put on and away went my small amount of air for the air brakes, leaving me with absolutely none. I had to approach my stations cautiously and stop her with the reverse. The conductor had safeguarded himself. He had not brought out any train carrying passengers without cutting in brakes quite according to Hoyle. I rather suspect this was deliberate since they gave me no assistance whatever in the switching operations. They wouldn't set a hand brake until I'd stopped the car. However, we did all the switching over the whole division, so nobody could grumble.

I had two more tricky propositions yet to face: the C.P.R. grade crossing and our own main line junction, the second of these approached by a steep little drop. I took no chances with either of these, but made sure that I could stop a safe distance back. I'd just brought her to a stand — and well clear — at the junction when Number Two went by at about seventy mph. Even then our troubles weren't quite over. I had warned my fireman to keep a good high water level in the boiler for fear of such a situation, and a few miles before reaching Biggar it came to pass. Both our injectors failed as the depleted water pressure could no longer force its way through the strainers owing to the grass which had gone in with the snow we had shovelled.

It is a very stringent regulation that incoming engines must be left on the ashpit with a good high level of water in the boiler. Since we got there with only three inches and no more available until the strainers had been cleaned out, I directed my fireman to see the hostler personally and acquaint him with the situation; I myself remaining with the engine until someone from the shop relieved me. Presently one of the wipers came out, a frightened lad who asked me to spot her at the water tank for him, as he was afraid to move her without any brake. I did this but I warned him that he had better get the hostler personally. Then and not until then, I booked in and made my way to the bunkhouse, the exiles' temporary home.

Next morning the whole establishment seemed to be resounding with roars for "Roe! The foreman wants to see him right away." I found him at last, irascible and bellowing, demanding to know what the hell I meant by bringing in an engine in that condition and walking off and leaving her like that! By now I was as angry as he was, and asked him not at all politely where he got that from. Apparently this was the hostler's report. I said, "Fetch him in here, then." "Nothing doing!" The man had something else to do than to run after me. I answered him, "The man had plenty of spare time to fill you up with a string of lies and you and he both have got time to listen to what I've got to say. If you haven't, I won't say another word here. I'll lay the whole case before the Master Mechanic." Seeing me determined, I expect he thought he'd better play safe. He called in the hostler, who also attempted to bluster but by the time I'd detailed the circumstances, together with the mention of my two witnesses, the case wore a different aspect. Later he was overheard dealing faithfully with the hostler. Some months later I received five Merit Marks for bringing in a train conveying passengers with only partial operation of air brakes. Not even the Company dared to acknowledge my bringing it in with brakes totally inoperative for fear of repercussions from the Railway Commission.

Some years later in the fearful winter of 1927 I had an experience that might have proved disastrous but fortunately did not. On the very last day of that year, New Year's Eve, I was called for the fast Coast Freight, due to leave at 4:30 a.m. I was told there was trouble up the road and we might be delayed. My fireman, a spare man like myself, was a young fellow whom I liked very much, not at all robust but a good fireman. It was fifty-eight degrees below that morning and the train felt like coupling onto the Rocky Mountains. I told the yardmaster he would need some additional power to get me out of the yard. He was one of the aforementioned 'office men', though a good man later. He said, "You're not even trying to!" I answered back, "No, and I don't intend to 'try' as you call it. The company expects this tender of coal to take her to Edson. [There was no halfway coaling plant then.] I'm not going to ruin my mate's fire and waste a couple of tons of coal for nothing by what you call 'trying'. I might as well try to push the mountains over." Eventually three big engines got us out over the first uphill mile. We had the prescribed thirty-three percent reduction of tonnage for temperatures of forty-five degrees or more below zero, so we got along fairly well.

The operator's block was on (that is, red) for further orders, and I climbed down to look around my engine. To my horror I found the second (reserve) injector on my side was frozen hard! It had been properly set for steam heating but either the vibration had shut it off, or I myself might have touched it inadvertently with my elbow and closed it thus. It had in any case to be thawed, not merely for immediate service if required but in the eighty miles before we reached our terminal the intense frost could split steel and even copper piping with unpleasant consequences to F.G.R.

Alas! In disconnecting the hosebag joint between engine and tender I found (when too late!) that the cut-out valve on the tender hadn't shut off and wouldn't and after clearing the ice from the hosebag my fireman and myself got drenched to the skin before we could re-establish the pipe joint. True, the water wasn't cold, but it was sunrise and fifty-eight degrees below zero! We were two sheets of ice in no time. Fortunately our engine was safe, and we saw the brakeman approaching whom I asked to take charge of her till we returned. We each had a heavy mackinaw coat to throw over us and we had to drag-leg back forty car lengths to the station and stand in front of a white hot stove before we could peel our now sodden garments off. We were going to be lucky to escape pneumonia! I think I was more afraid for my fireman than I was for myself since he was known for a delicate fellow, which I never was. Actually, neither of us ever turned a hair.

But our troubles were not yet over. We were given orders to Gainford only. An eastbound fellow was off the track there, and we were to help him on again. This proved to be something of an understatement. He was off the track and the track itself was invisible underneath a sort of rough-and-ready skating rink. The pump house was down by the lake, half a mile or more from the water tank, and the depth of water was shown by a ball attached to a float in the tank. Through some oversight the old pumpman had allowed the tank to overflow and the whole adjacent area was under some inches of ice. This eastbound drag stopping to take water, was lifted bodily above the grip of her flanges on the rails and when we got there was fifty or sixty degrees crosswise of the track and utterly helpless.

It was fortunate for ourselves that the exercises before the white hot stove and the subsequent slow pull of some fifteen miles had warmed and dried us thoroughly. For the next seven hours or so I sat at the window in that aching cold, pulling and pushing, and backing and filling, chained or coupled at long range or short to the eastbound engine; taking the handsignals of her tail end crew (whom her own engineer couldn't see) and translating them by steam whistle for his guidance into joint action by our combined forces; gaining a fractional toehold by one move and perhaps losing it by the next until at last after an eternity of doubts, disputes, deliberations and decisions, we heard the music of the familiar 'clank' as she settled down on the steel which the toiling sectionmen had prepared for her reception. It was now around 7 p.m.

By this time there were four or five trains gathered here, all of them pretty well frozen up. This time we had a bit of an edge on things. We were a red card precedence freight, twelve hours late and seventy miles from our terminal. Our train had been left on a falling grade so we got away with little difficulty. The other fellows helped one another away. How the last of all got clear I never did learn. Probably by giving up his train or a portion of it. We ourselves reached Edson about 11 p.m. after what seemed like a luxury run, compared with the manifold miseries of our twenty-two hour day.

Next morning, New Year's Day, we were called for 6 a.m. Our brakeman told us we were being held until the arrival of Number One, who'd 'pulled a lung' (that is, drawgear) on the diner at Carrot Creek tank. We were getting eighteen cars of coal, about forty percent of tonnage. It was sixty below zero. Now and again I moved my engine back or forward slightly to limber her gears a little against freezing up. It was 11 a.m. before Number One arrived. The brakeman cut off six cars to see if she could move them: not a move! Then three: they wouldn't stir. I finally tore one car loose. It required two additional engines bigger than mine to lift the eighteen cars. Once we got them going, however, they were a mere fleabite; and the 5151 being a passenger engine we trotted them up hill and down dale in capital style. We were in Edmonton by 4 p.m. in good time for New Year's Evening.

It must be understood that such episodes as the foregoing are not to be misconceived as 'accidents' in any real sense of the term. Even apart from there being no human casualties, there was nothing about them of any dramatic interest that could arrest the attention of a reporter from the standpoint of 'news'. A late train — unless it happens to be a Royal one or something similar — or a derailment has nothing specially remarkable about it. In most cases any significance it possesses would be missed entirely by anyone not closely familiar with railroad rules and working which is something very few reporters exhibit in their descriptions of railroad occurrences. They are simply such incidental happenings as occur to most of us in our daily lives. The world of automobile has familiarized us with the fact that an accident is frequently something where once in a hundred times some everyday practice or experience just failed to 'click' and a casualty results. The one obvious feature about the foregoing is that they couldn't have occurred in summer. Actually the only serious accident to happen to me in thirty-five years of railroading occurred in the summertime under the most placidly favourable conditions conceivable.

Like many other, I'd been 'set back' firing in the hungry thirties of the depression years. This night I was on the yard with an arthritic little Frenchman who could scarcely give her a light throttle for a slow movement. I sometimes had to take over for that purpose. About all he could do was to yank her well open and shut her again at once. I was putting in a fire when he had to do this. She seemed to bound forward and then prop, like a horse on its heels, and I started to slide across the deck toward the boiler head. I grabbed for the tender and it really seemed as though one-half of me stopped and the other half kept going. I walked home that night somewhat stiff, and was not much different in the morning. Since there were two or three days coming to me for 'excess miles' my wife suggested my taking them now. By the second morning it would have

181

Snowplough

required a block and tackle to get me out of bed. I had to have ten stitches in my back and was off duty from August until April.

But it would be fundamentally misleading and almost in a sense ungrateful to concentrate exclusively upon the wintry aspects of the railroad life. The cab of a steam locomotive could certainly be a hot spot in the summertime, but on the move we could trim it to suit ourselves and make it almost anything we desired. And one can never forget the beautiful evenings and mornings on some of the night runs. Although one never forgot his eternal loyalties to the common truism that 'anytime is a good time to be coming in', and although we preferred a clear dark still night as our ideal, yet some of the brilliant moonlight nights were so utterly beautiful that we almost regretted coming to the end of the run. I worked a good deal on fast runs that would leave in the evening and be back next morning by six or seven with just time enough if we were on time for the very smallest of the 'wee sma' hours' to ease our eyes with a couple of hours in bed. In the height of summer we would be leaving just at the break of dawn and the non-stop journey home across the varied panorama of the prairie division with the early sun at our backs was an unbroken delight!

Some of the truly spectacular mountain dawns and sunsets would have needed the pen of a Ruskin to describe them. Different from those innocents who promise themselves "some really good pictures on the way through" (and may never see a peak) we viewed them under all conditions. Cold sharp days were the best. But to see the endless variation of the mountain clefts and gorges changing even in the very act of gazing upon them as the climbing sun gained higher levels and slanted farther to the right; to see (it took place too rapidly for any need to watch) rift or canyon changing from deep indigo, mauve or magenta to the most delicate of rose pinks, and finally to old gold and sun white, was an experience not soon to be forgotten.

From a totally different angle, however, the mountains had curious repercussions among the men. One seldom seemed to meet anyone who viewed them from any neutral, middle of the road standpoint. We used to say that you either couldn't get a man into them or you couldn't get him out! They certainly had two enormous attractions for an engineman. Mountain water was incomparable, one hundred percent for boiler purposes. You could carry a 'pot-full' almost 'out of sight in the top of the glass'. This reserve was a tremendous advantage in times of emergency or when coming to a tank as we sometimes did 'with all the water in the boiler'. With the enormously hot super-steamers of the latter days, a glassful of water could disappear with appalling rapidity if you had to make a run for a tank!

The second attraction was — no blizzards! We have seen something of what that could mean on the baldheaded plains. Although there were everywhere occasional tanks of good water even in the very worst of the alkali areas, most of the water in the plains regions didn't deserve the name; we called it 'wet air'. Some was beautiful water to drink; some was as deadly outside a boiler as it was in. Until the railway companies began treating it (which only partially alleviated it), men would make an entire division without daring to carry the water high enough to show in the water glass. Under such conditions, to scorch a crown-sheet was by no means the instant dismissal offence that it was in the good water territories. Circumstances were taken into account, as they should be. It might be wondered why men were willing to remain in service on such divisions as many preferred to.

Speaking for myself (as one of them) I never cared for a territory where your only chance to see a mile was to lie on your back and look up and where a rock the size of a barn might be waiting for you round the next corner. I once fired an all night run from Edmonton to Jasper, two hundred and forty miles, for some months. This was from harvest time to about Christmas. I was soon wearied of rocks, torrents and coniferous woods, not to mention stretches of scrub and swampy muskeg. I happened to mention to my mate, a not particularly imaginative man, that the first fifty miles west of Edmonton with their cultivated farms, were my preferred territory and found him to be of the very same opinion.

24

Conclusion

I am nearing the end of the trail. As I look back over the thirty-five years of railroading which, officially, terminated my working career and the years have in some measure at least brought the power to look before and after: it is amusing to compare ourselves as we were with ourselves as we thought we were. I am reminded at the moment of an engineer with whom I fired for some considerable time. He was one of the most imperturbable fellows I ever worked with. He had a saying of his own that was never out of his mouth for long: "The main thing is not to worry." I must do him the justice to say that the phrase was more than just a catchword. He lived it at all times and on one crucial occasion at least, if the officials knew what we knew, we would have been summarily fired and he had seven children.

This formula appealed to me.   Not for its inherent philosophy; I wasn't old enough in the service to rise to these heights. It did, however, seem a splendid cloak under which a new hand could masquerade as a seasoned old head. Even if I was inwardly sweating blood it was, I felt, due to my professional aplomb to utter this ritual in order to show my sheer unconcern. At first the parrot-like refrain was just that and nothing more but in time it began to burn itself in under the skin. When this happened I began to think it as well as say it. I don't mean to suggest that I never worried anymore but the occasions for this certainly became fewer particularly after I became an engineer. By this time I had learned to distinguish between mere worry and sensible precautions before starting out.

If a road breakdown occurred, the Fates almost certainly ordained the engineer in the case, my engineer, would be some well-upholstered old veteran who simply couldn't crawl under her. I recall one heavily thawing winter day when I lay on my back in melting snow for over two hours trying to loosen some recalcitrant nuts that would fall off fast enough without warning but couldn't be disconnected by human agency without something more than prayer and fasting. The anti-worrying philosophy was heavily drawn upon in some cases. Many of the men who were too fat to crawl in under her wouldn't show up till they were due off the shop track. They would then throw their ditty bag up on the deck and yell: "Are ya jake to go?" and take a chance on the engine being all in one piece. I'd done my firing for promotion, passed my exams, and put in three winters driving before I ever saw a breakdown and the same old fraud let me in for two of them in as many months.

I adopted a technique of my own with that man. I showed up fifteen or twenty minutes ahead of the (paid) preparatory time and went round her myself with the required inspection. Sometimes when I was peering underneath her some clown would query me in scorn: "Going to rebuild her Frank?" I would answer him: "Not here. The Company'll do it for me here. Perhaps you would sooner do it yourself out in the road in six feet of snow." Our only responsibility before leaving was to notice and report any defects which the shop must rectify. Once we left the shop track the responsibility was solely ours.

I tried to stay ahead of trouble and by virtue of such 'manners and customs' as these I managed to retain the not worrying creed as a principle and also follow it as a practice. In the thirty-five years of railroad service I stared out of cab windows for the equivalent of forty-seven times around the globe. I fired for one hundred and thirty-nine engineers and two hundred and eight firemen fired for me. I have good reason to believe that when I retired on my sixty-fifth birthday on the friendliest terms, I had neither injured any other man's self-respect nor forfeited my own.

I have been asked more than once if I would care to live my life over again. Perhaps there are few of us who have not more or less idly speculated on this question among friends. Perhaps the impossibility of such a process reflects itself in the equal impossibility of an answer in any categorical Yes or No.

If I were called upon to face such a contingency there are certain provisos I would like to stipulate beforehand. I have never had any desire to evade hard work; I have never at any time regretted the years of hard physical toil. There are two principal reasons for this — respectively physical and psychological. We have all known those men whose life careers were cast in sedentary occupations but who upon retirement were simply going to pull trees up. By the time these men retire it quickly becomes apparent that they simply haven't got the staying power. In some tragic cases they've pushed themselves over the limit and died before they'd been free very long. I have long been of the opinion that 'exercise muscles' are no substitute for 'hard work muscles'. My farmer chum's brother commonly paid his western visits in harvest time. He boasted a conspicuous pair of biceps, real YMCA stuff, and viewed our puny display with scorn. However, in a couple of hours he was invalided from the field in utter exhaustion while we could pitch grain sheaves all day and never turn a hair.

The psychological reason is this: I don't think it is good for anyone to grow up in ignorance of how the toilers of the world live. Even in this later age of automation it is even more imperative if the person is likely to occupy a post of authority later on. On a vast business enterprise like a railroad, no one could be master of all its varied skills, but he should know some of the lowlier ones. A deceased friend of mine, the head of an important university faculty, whose own experience of the 'black squad' came about from an irresponsible recklessness in youth, counted those years among the most formative and valuable of his life. He also thought that some such training should be obligatory upon all academics. Within our own time the movement of the 'worker priests' in France and a similar urge now gaining strength among the Anglican clergy in England show that my friend's views are not wholly those of one crying in the wilderness.

It was something of a truism on the railroads, based on a certain degree of truth, that all retired railroaders were miserable, unhappy men. I have known such. After my own retirement I ran across an old passenger man, for whom I had fired, coming off work as watchman with his dinner pail and not at all looking like an 'aristocrat of labour'.

Pursuant to this orthodox creed, my very last fireman asked me if I thought I could take it after I dropped out. I said: "Don't worry about me taking it." "Aw, yes, that's what they all say. I bet you after about a week you'll be crawling around the Foreman, ready to hand in your pension for a job." "Different here, my son, among other matters I've got about four books to write." When he recovered from the shock he acknowledged there might be exceptions to the rule.

I don't know that I'd have it much otherwise . . .

Glossary

Air brakes: brake system found on locomotives and rolling stock usually classed as a system of continuous brakes operated by compressed air.

Air hose: flexible hose arranged with a coupling at each end by means of which the brake piping is readily connected between engine, tender and cars.

Alkali regions: regions in which soluble mineral salts or a mixture of soluble salts are present in the soil and water. In western Canada these areas may be found in parts of southern Alberta and Saskatchewan.

Boiler washer: roundhouse worker who flushes out the internal water spaces in the locomotive boiler.

Bonanza farming: a type of farming of very large areas. One such farm in Canada was 6,000 acres while in California there was one of 18,000 acres.

Boomer: an itinerant railroad worker — those people roamed all over North America working for various railway lines.

Carrying green: a regularly scheduled train running in two or more sections. All sections but the last had to signify there were other sections following by means of green flags carried on the front of the locomotive.

Chipman Ranch: established in 1882 by the Chipman Ranche Company and was located where the city of Calgary now stands.

Coulter (colter): a sharp blade or wheel attached to the beam of a plough used to cut the ground in advance of the ploughshare.

189

Crown sheet: a large section of boiler plate directly over the fire and forming the roof of the locomotive firebox. In case of low water in the boiler this is the first part of the boiler to be damaged.

Derail: a safety device placed on the track in order to automatically derail any rolling stock that attempts to move over it.

Distributing valve: the principal feature of the Westinghouse ET locomotive brake equipment. It performs the functions of the older triple valve along with several features that make brake applications faster and more efficient.

Drag: a made-up freight train.

Drivers (driving wheel): any one of the wheels under a locomotive which transfers the power developed in the locomotive cylinders to tractive effort.

Dynamo: a small steam driven electric generator that supplied power for the lights on a steam locomotive. It was normally fitted just forward of the locomotive cab on top of the boiler.

Emergency stop: an emergency application of the air brake carried out in one of several ways. It could be initiated by the locomotive engineer or train conductor, or automatically by a broken brake pipe or air hose.

Extra gang: workmen who work on various special sections of track as opposed to the regular section gang who maintain one specific section of track.

Falling down for steam: a locomotive that could not maintain steam pressure and was therefore immobile. This was usually the result of running out of boiler feed water.

Foreign engine: a locomotive maintained in another roundhouse. For example, an engine running from the Lakehead to Winnipeg was considered a foreign engine at Winnipeg.

Green coal: a term normally used in conjunction with 'green fire' in which the glowing firebed of a locomotive was completely covered with fresh coal. This was a splendid producer of thick, black smoke with little heat.

Highball: colloquial term for the signal to move out. The term stems from the days when the signal was literally a large ball moving up or down a shaft on a signal tower.

Hogger/hoghead: colloquial terms for a locomotive engineer.

Injector: device for delivering water into the pressure side of the boiler. Injectors were therefore most important as well as tricky to operate.

Jungle terminals: a terminal at one of the smaller, isolated prairie towns. In the early years of this century there were few or no amenities at any of these points.

Kicker: a sticking triple valve; this caused much trouble for all concerned and could be dangerous.

Live engine: locomotive with steam pressure on the boiler.

Locomotive foreman: the official in charge of a roundhouse, normally a machinist by trade.

Locomotive hostler: the employee responsible for moving locomotives in and out of the roundhouse and making all the engine movements required by the locomotive foreman for maintenance, etc.

Locomotive reverse gear: the mechanism by means of which the direction of the locomotive is reversed. It was also used to lessen the amount of steam used in every stroke of the piston in order to increase efficiency.

Lodge: an agricultural term meaning to beat down or lay flat, as vegetation in a storm.

Longstroker: an engineer who failed to shorten the stroke of the steam inlet valve in order to reduce the amount of steam admitted to the piston at high speeds. This failure resulted in a large reduction of locomotive efficiency and caused much extra work for the locomotive fireman. (See locomotive reverse gear.)

Mallet: a large type of articulated steam locomotive — very little used in Canada.

Master mechanic: a railroad official one step above the locomotive foreman. His responsibilities extended over a division or district.

Missouri coteau: the hilly upland region extending from Montana into southern Alberta.

Mixed (mixed freight): a train made up of both passenger and freight cars.

Oil car: an oil storage car that was kept heated in order to store the various engine oils in a more fluid state than they would be at ambient temperatures — a necessity in a prairie winter.

Plough, breaking (also prairie breaker): a large, heavily constructed plough specially designed to cut the tough prairie sod; it was always provided with a coulter.

Plugging her: closing the steam throttle on the locomotive — usually an emergency movement in this context.

Pot-full: a high level of water in the locomotive boiler.

Put the gun on: starting the locomotive steam injector to feed water into the boiler.

Rule G: a section of the railroad *Operating Rules* which stated: "The use of intoxicants by employees while on duty is prohibited. Their use, or the frequenting of places where they are sold, is sufficient cause for dismissal."

Second crop (back-setting): an agricultural term referring to the second ploughing. This ploughing was normally carried out prior to sowing the first wheat crop.

Slow order: a speed restriction placed on any railroad rolling stock passing over certain designated lengths of track because of new construction, damage to roadbed, etc.

Spot: to move a piece of railway rolling stock to a certain certain position, 'spot', on the track.

Stool: an agricultural term meaning to put forth shoots from the base or root; sowing thinly facilitates this development.

Tonnage rating: an adjustable index of the hauling power of a given locomotive taking into account the calculated tractive force of the locomotive, the condition of the roadbed, the temperature, and the makeup of the train to be pulled.

Train order: an official, written directive authorizing the movement of a train, locomotive or any other specialized vehicle using the rail lines beyond the yard limits.

Triple valve: a valve in the airbrake system of older locomotives which applies and releases the brakes according to various pressures in the train line.

Turn-around end: the terminal at which a locomotive is taken off one train and returns to its original starting point pulling another train. (See 'foreign engine'.)

Whistle my green: a whistle signal between the front end crews of two trains one of which was running in sections. This signal indicated that the crew of the other train was aware that there was more than one section of the first train. (See 'carrying green'.)

Wye: a section of track shaped like the letter 'Y' that enabled a locomotive to be turned around.

Publications by Frank Gilbert Roe

"After Fifty Years." *The New Trail.* University of Alberta Quarterly, October 1944, pp. 157-161.

"The Alberta Wet Cycle of 1899-1903." *Agricultural History,* Vol. 28, 1954, pp. 112-120.

"Buffalo and Snow." *The Canadian Historical Review,* Vol. XVII, June 1936, 125-146.

"Buffalo as a Possible Influence in the Development of Prairie Lands." *The Canadian Historical Review,* Vol. XX, 1939, 275-287.

"Buffalo Trails and Fur Posts." *Queens Quarterly,* Vol. LXVII, 1960, 449-461.

"Convocation Address." *The New Trail.* University of Alberta Quarterly, Fall 1951, pp. 166-172.

"The 'Crooked Field'." *Antiquity,* Vol. X, September 1936, 325-340.

"A Day in Court." *Alberta Historical Review,* Vol. 20, No. 3, 1972, 1-5.

"Duty." *Royal Canadian Mounted Police Quarterly,* October 1937.

"Early Agriculture in Western Canada in Relation to Climactic Stability." *Agricultural History,* Vol. 26, 1952, 104-123.

"Early Opinion on the 'Fertile Belt' of Western Canada." *Canadian Historical Review,* Vol. XXVII, 1946, 131-149.

"Edmonton a Century Ago." *Alberta Historical Review,* Vol. 12, 1964, 10-16.

"The Extermination of the Buffalo in Western Canada." *Canadian Historical Review,* Vol. XV, 1934, 1-23, 213-218.

" 'Forests' and Woods in Mediaeval England." *Transactions of the Royal Society of Canada,* Vol. XLIX, 1955, Section II, 67-93.

"From Dogs to Horses Among the Western Indian Tribes." *Transactions of the Royal Society of Canada,* Vol XXXIII, 1939, Section II, 209-275.

"The Hudson's Bay Company and the Indians." *The Beaver,* September 1936, pp. 8-14, 64-65.

"I Saw Three Englands." *The Railway Magazine,* Vol. 95, January-March 1949, 7-12, 81-86.

The Indian and the Horse. Norman, Okalahoma: University of Oklahoma Press, 1955.

"The Lake Edith Railway." *Canadian National Railways Magazine,* April 1937, pp. 9-13, 23.

"The Legend of the Bad Indian." *The Victoria Naturalist,* Vol. 13, No. 3, September 1956.

"The Marlowe Fiasco." *Queen's Quarterly,* Vol. XLIV, 1957, 89-100.

The North American Buffalo. Toronto: University of Toronto Press, 1951.

"The Numbers of the Buffalo." *Transactions of the Royal Society of Canada,* Vol. XXXI, 1937, Section II, 171-203.

"The Old Log House in Western Canada." *Alberta Historical Review,* Vol. 6, No. 2, 1958, 1-9.

"The Oxford of Our Province." *The New Trail.* University of Alberta Quarterly, April 1944, pp. 49-51.

"Period Piece." *Queen's Quarterly,* Vol. LXIX, 1963, 601-606.

"Pilgrim at Glastonbury." *Queen's Quarterly,* Vol. LXV, 1958, 650-663.

"The Red River Hunt." *Transactions of the Royal Society of Canada,* Vol XXIX, 1935, Section II, 171-217.

"Remittance Men." *Alberta Historical Review,* Vol. 2, No. 1, 1954; rpt. 1970.

"The Sod House." *Alberta Historical Review,* Vol. 18, No. 3, 1970, 1-7.

"Some Historical Evidence on the Earlier Physiography of the North American Prairies." *Transactions of the Royal Society of Canada,* Vol. LV, 1961, Section II, 9-35.

"An Unsolved Problem of Canadian History." *Canadian Historical Association Annual Report,* 1936, pp. 65-77.

"Victoria Day and the Victorians." *Edmonton Journal,* May 24, 1943.

"A Week in Southern Ireland." *Queen's Quarterly,* Vol. LXVI, 1959, 450-467.

"Western Penetration of the Historic Buffalo in the Upper Bow River Valley." *Alberta Historical Review,* Vol. 5, 1957, 21-24.

"What is a 'Field'?" *Transactions of the Royal Society of Canada,* Vol. L, 1956, Section II, 21-37.

"White Buffalo." *Transactions of the Royal Society of Canada,* Vol. XXXVIII, 1944, Section II, 155-173.

"The 'Wild Animal Path' Origin of Ancient Roads." *Antiquity,* Vol.III, 1929, 299-311.

"The Winding Road." *Antiquity*, Vol. XIII, June 1939, 191-206.

Index